IT'S NEVER
OK TO
KISS
THE
INTERVIEWER

IT'S NEVER OK TO KISS THE INTERVIEWER

...AND OTHER SECRETS TO SURVIVING, THRIVING AND HIGH FIVING AT WORK

JANE SUNLEY

LONDON   MADRID
NEW YORK   MEXICO CITY
BOGOTA   BUENOS AIRES
BARCELONA   MONTERREY

Published by
LID Publishing Ltd
The Loft, 19a Floral Street
Covent Garden
London WC2E 9DS
United Kingdom
info@lidpublishing.com
www.lidpublishing.com

A member of:

BPR
Business Publishers Roundtable

www.businesspublishersroundtable.com

Printed by CPI Group (UK) Ltd.

ISBN: 978-1-907794-60-5

Cover and page design: Laura Hawkins

THIS BOOK IS DEDICATED TO:

INDIA & LILY

— IN THE HOPE YOU WILL
ALWAYS LOVE YOUR JOBS

CONTENTS:

ACKNOWLEDGEMENTS   09

WHAT'S RIGHT FOR YOU:

01   Why bother?   11

02   The career cycle
       – deciding where you are and what's next   13

03   Start with the end in mind   17

04   Your values   20

05   So what do you want to do and where
       do you want to do it?   25

06   Experience along the way   29

07   Changing jobs and making those
       all-important decisions   35

08   The departure lounge   39

MAKING IT HAPPEN:

09   Your CV   45

10   How to apply   51

11   Prepping for interviews   56

12   The generation game and why it matters   61

13   Being the best 'you' you can be   66

14   The power of mentoring   71

15   Becoming a mentor   78

16   Confidence, poise and the X factor   81

17   Assertiveness – time to man up   84

18   Standing out from the crowd   89

19   Follow-up   94

20   Tests, assessments and other tricky stuff   97

21 Accepting a role   105

22 Preparing to start   108

TWO-THIRDS THROUGH... WORDS   112

THRIVING, SURVIVING, HIGH-FIVING:

23 Your first day – agreeing the ground rules   114

24 Building reputation   120

25 Stamina   125

26 Communication   128

27 Guidance, support and feedback   134

28 Bullying, bitching and belligerent bosses   139

29 Reviewing your progress   145

30 Leadership must-haves (even if you're not one)   148

31 Getting stuff done and a sense of urgency   152

32 Enthusiasm and motivation   157

33 Learning and progression   162

34 Team dynamics and having fun   167

35 What you need to do next –
how to get the best out of this book   172

36 Why listen to me?   174

ACKNOWLEDGEMENTS:

EMILY PERRY for her always helpful editing.

DAVID WOODS for championing this book.

HOLLY EDWARDS for providing Gen Y feedback.

MY COLLEAGUES AT PURPLE CUBED
for their never-ending support and inspiration.

WHAT'S RIGHT FOR **YOU:**

| **01** | WHY **BOTHER?**

There will always be demand for talented people. Regardless of the state of the economy and media reports of rising numbers of jobless people, talent will out; if you've got the goods, you'll get the job. Now there's an interesting prospect…

Pretty much everyone is talented in one way or another. The key is to identify and nurture your talent; this is easier to do if you pursue something you love doing. You might think it wouldn't be all that difficult to find a job you like and then do well in it. Maybe it was that way in the past. But now there are so many variables that the smart people (and you're one of them if you've picked up this book) are shortening the odds by actively making themselves more marketable as a job seeker and more compelling as an employee.

This book is about standing out from the crowd in the right way; definitely in a way that is appropriate to the situation.

Like award-winning athletes or performers, job seekers today need to prepare; train, if you like, in order to stand out from the thousands of other applicants. How can an employer know what you can do for them if you don't point it out?

It's like the man who built the best phone app ever, then didn't market it – lost in a sea of mediocrity when it could have made him millions.

So this book, in part, is a crash course in marketing yourself. You owe it to yourself to be the best 'you' that you can possibly be. It's also about focusing your efforts on the right things that will make you happy and that you will enjoy (because we all do things better if we like them), therefore helping you to achieve your version of success.

This book will be invaluable in helping you to sort through the inconsistent messages, conflicting advice and massive information flow; it gets down to basics – what you want, how you're going to get there and, most importantly, how to know when you're on track. It won't freak you out or expect you to be someone you're not. And there's no fluffy weirdness – this is all about simple, straightforward career planning and personal focus with improvements that anyone can make.

A **TRUE** STORY:

A student I mentored, let's call her Kate, was just about to graduate and was look-ing for her ideal role. Kate is bright, organized, sensible, mature, she had worked part-time jobs throughout university so had good, relevant experience – all in all a fab potential employee. However, she lacked confidence; this showed in the way she presented herself. She felt thoroughly intimidated by every interviewer and so went to pieces every time. This fateful combo was stopping her from landing her dream job. By adopting some of the simple tools and techniques in this book she landed her ultimate dream job. And now she is very, very good at it. Hurrah!

IF YOU ONLY DO **THREE THINGS:**

1 Start thinking now about what career happiness might 'look like' for you.
2 Start thinking right now about how you can stand out from the crowd.
3 Remember that the people you work for or might potentially work for are only people just like you (and, maybe not so long ago, they were right where you are now).

02 | THE CAREER CYCLE – DECIDING WHERE YOU ARE AND WHAT'S NEXT

By 'career' I don't mean going off on a commuter train in a suit to a 9-5. In its broadest sene, career is defined by the good old Oxford English Dictionary as "a person's course or progress through life (or a distinct portion of life)".

Your path could potentially take you in a myriad of different directions, and that's why it's sometimes difficult to know which way to go on this road through life. One of the functions of this book is to help find some good options for you, as an individual, and help you make some great decisions.

Your career is not about what your parents/teachers/partner/family/friends (all 995 of them on Facebook) want. No doubt they can (and will be very willing to) give advice and guidance – I'm not suggesting you ignore this. The problem with listening to advice, though, is that so often it's conflicting, leaving you unclear and worrying about letting all of those well-meaning people down.

FOR THOSE WHO like the detail and/or are interested in the history of language, the term 'career' comes from the 16th-century French word *carriere* which means road. This in turn comes from the Latin *via cararia*, meaning a track for a wheeled vehicle (or literally a road for wagons). Like any road you happen to find yourself upon, it's important to know where you're trying to get to and roughly how you're going to get there. And once you're on the right road, you can progress onto the career highway and maybe even the career superhighway. That would be pretty fantastic.

If you're at a stage in your career where you want to progress, make a difference and, ultimately, be happy at work, then it's important to start with the end in mind. However, in the real world, unless you are an exceptionally enlightened, that's not always apparent. So first it's important to identify what stage in the 'career cycle' you're at now.

WHAT STAGE ARE YOU AT NOW?

0-12:
THE EARLY YEARS
(formative)

IN EDUCATION/
DEVELOPMENT

FURTHER
EDUCATION

FIRST ROLE
(and
subsequent roles)

THE **CAREER** SUPERHIGHWAY...

1. THE EARLY YEARS 0-12: most people don't think of their formative years as part of their career, yet the experiences you have and what you learn at school and outside it will surely start to form the basis of your future road through life. You might have noticed a few role models who inspire you.

2. IN EDUCATION or development: by the time you choose your subject options in school (or decide not to do some of them), you'll already be starting to form ideas about what interests you, what topics and activities you like and how you might be able to use this in your future career. People go to work for a good many years so it makes sense to find something you enjoy. Now's the time to start thinking about what that might 'look like'.

3. FURTHER EDUCATION: if you go down this route, you'll still be having lots of stimulus around what you like and how you might like to take this forward. If by now you still have no idea what you're going to do with your degree in philosophy, pure maths or politicizing Beyoncé (yes you can) — and many people don't — it's time to start thinking through all the options, trying out some part-time work, work placements and networking. It's also time to work on the practical, everyday, essential skills and attributes described in this book. The chances are, though, that you won't learn them in all but the most enlightened of educational establishments (one day maybe...)

4. FIRST ROLE: hurrah, you made it — we really hope you're enjoying it. If you're reading this book, the chances are you're either ambitious and always thinking about your next move, or things aren't quite as you expected; you're not as happy or engaged as you'd like to be - or maybe somewhere in between.

5. LEARNING AND PROGRESSING: this is a catch-all for all of the stages in your career where you're feeling good and feeling you can work towards where you want to be. You might still be in your first or subsequent roles; the point is, you feel you are working towards where you ultimately want to be.

6. HAPPY, ENGAGED AND GENERALLY 'ON A ROLL': things are going well, you're feeling satisfied and fulfilled and know what your next progression will be.

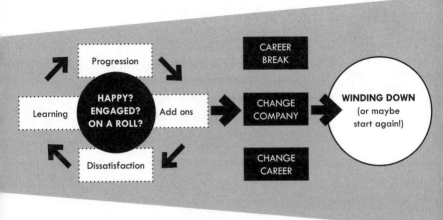

7. ADD-ONS: when you're at the (7) stage you might want to think about some additional activities to a) develop b) pass on knowledge c) give back – or all three. Think CSR (corporate social responsibility) activities – making the world a better place, giving back, caring for the environment, such as taking on a work-experience student, mentoring, non-executive directorships, sabbaticals for travel or charitable work – whatever floats your boat and helps you keep motivated and excited about your career.

8. DISSATISFIED: it starts off as mild irritation. Before you know it, you wake up one morning and you're just plain unhappy at work. Sometimes this situation prevails for a long time (years in some cases). It's not good for your health, those closest to you or for the organization and colleagues you work with, so be honest and brave – do something to change it.

9. CAREER BREAK: this might be enforced or by choice. Either way, getting back onto the career road can be challenging. You might have lost a bit of confidence, need to update your skills or want to reassess your options.

10. CHANGE OF COMPANY: you like your chosen career path but you're thinking about moving on from the organization you're with. Use your energy to see if you can bring about the necessary changes. Talk to the person or people who can make this happen rather than putting your energy into griping about it. And if things don't improve, then start thinking about how you can move on.

11. CHANGE OF CAREER: for many reasons, career changes happen at all stages of the journey. If you're not clear on the what and how, find a trusted advisor who can talk though your reasoning and options with you or invest in some professional coaching. This might be someone you admire, a colleague, someone within your family or circle of friends – maybe even your best friend's dad.

12. WINDING DOWN: unless you're financially blessed, it's likely that this winding down period will occur towards your twilight years. By this stage you'll be passing on your expertise to others and planning how you're going to spend your time/remain fulfilled once your formal career has come to a close.

IF YOU ONLY DO **THREE THINGS:**

1 Work out where you're at on the career life cycle and what your next step will be.
2 Take responsibility for your choices and start working out the options and decisions.
3 Remember you have a right to be happy at work – it should never be something to be endured under sufferance – life really is too short.

03 | START WITH THE **END IN MIND**

In a world where information flow is super-fast and the only constant is change – at the time of writing, there are almost 300 billion emails sent daily with the average teenager, for example, sending 3000+ texts a month – it's difficult to plan ahead. However it's not impossible. The trick is to think 'big picture' and then fill in the details as you go.

Some fortunate people have an innate sense of where they want to go in life. For most, however, this is a journey that requires a lot of thought.

Sometimes people get hung up on an actual role or place they'd like to work. All of this is important but the key question is 'What do I want to get out of my career – and how do I want my career to affect my life?'

One technique you could try is to write yourself an epitaph: what would I one day like to be remembered for?

A TALE OF **TWO SISTERS:**

Mia had somehow known since she was small that she wanted to work with people and help them to solve their problems. As she grew up, this expanded into an aspiration to become a child psychologist. Focusing on this goal helped her choose her academic subject options, university, degree, employer, all the way through the cycle. Her desired epitaph might be: I made a difference by helping others.

Kellie, on the other hand, had a good idea of what she didn't want (a long, long list) and decided to wait and see what destiny dealt her. School was something of a challenge and she managed to get through it without much enthusiasm for her subjects. She knew she didn't want an academic career, favouring a more creative and practical approach. Convinced she'd be scouted as a model, she waited for fate to take a hand. She was out of work for a long time before she gave up on her dream and took a sales assistant role in a store where, with a lot more luck than is likely, she still might be spotted by a talent scout (one day…). Her desired epitaph might be: I was rich and famous.

It's unusual to be like Mia. However, if you're more like Kellie, you're in good company, so have a clear Plan A – work out the options and then work in a very focused way to get there. As a backup, it's possible and sensible to work out a Plan B in case things don't go your way. There is nothing wrong with wanting to be 'rich and famous', but it's important to note that the percentage of people to whom this happens, without a lot of effort and luck, is miniscule. The most important thing for anyone and everyone is to be specific about what your goal is and then you can work out what the HOW might look like.

HOW TO DECIDE YOUR GOALS:

- **THINK ABOUT:**
    - **A:** What you like doing
    - **B:** What skills you're using when doing the things you enjoy
    - **C:** What means a lot to you
    - **D:** What you are good at
    - **E:** What others admire about you (you'll probably have to ask them)
    - **F:** What sort of people you admire and why
    - **G:** What things you do that you're better at than others

- **DREAM IT**
    - ★ Think 10 years out (even though this might seem too far in the future).
    - ★ Have a quick daydream about what that might look like.

- ★ A good time to do this is when you're falling asleep in the evening or waking up in the morning.
- ★ If you're a visual person, imagine an oversized TV in your head and 'watch' yourself on that TV – what you're doing, where you are doing it…

O Or you might prefer to write down what you do and don't want.

O Keep it 'big picture': this is about the destination, not the journey.

O Avoid putting limits on your dreaming – the practical aspects can be worked out later.

O Ask yourself 'what would make me happy?'

If you're really stuck, find a trusted friend or family member to help you. Give them the list of questions above under 'Think about' and get them to 'interview you', probing for good responses.

Your goals will be influenced by your values so before you go any further, it's a good idea to read and digest Chapter 4.

IF YOU ONLY DO **THREE THINGS:**

1 Start from the premise 'most things are possible if I put the work in and do the right things'.
2 Avoid relying solely on fate (but don't ignore it either).
3 Work out your end goal.

|**04**| YOUR **VALUES**

Many organizations define their values – what they stand for, how they operate; they become culture.

Some organizations even live and breathe these values (think Facebook, Google, Apple and my business Purple Cubed).

APPLE'S CORE VALUE, said its eminent and sadly departed ex-CEO, Steve Jobs, is this: "We believe people with passion can change the world for the better... and that those people who are crazy enough to think they can change the world are the ones who actually do."

PURPLE CUBED'S VALUES:

Achievement, Freedom, Fun, Image, Relationships, Make it simple, Improvement with originality, Trust and integrity.

They make up quite a list when considering say "make it simple" – yet they're so fundamental to what we do and the way we do it that we wouldn't reduce them. Instead we use a mnemonic to remember them:

AFFIRM IT

If you're looking for a workplace where you can progress, make a contribution and enjoy yourself, it will certainly help if you know in advance what the employer stands for; how they 'do things around here'. And if they've made this clear, unambiguous and easy to relate to, then that tells you something about the way they run their business.

This is only half the story. This book is about you and how you can be happy and successful (whatever that means to you;

the individual). This will be whole lot easier if you define and understand your key strengths together with your personal values. Then you can find somewhere where your values and theirs are ALIGNED.

This is not fluffy 'business speak'. It's just common sense – if you know what you're looking for, you'll be more likely to achieve it.

So, here's the good bit…

HOW TO DEFINE

YOUR PERSONAL VALUES:

Take a blank piece of paper (Or even better, go to the my website www.janesunley.com, where there's a free, really nifty bit of kit that will make this exercise super easy - and a bit more fun - for you).

1   Sit somewhere quiet where you won't be interrupted and think about everything that's important to you about work (I've resisted the urge to 'give examples in a box below' because this is about you, not me nor the rest of the world).
2   As these thoughts come into your head, jot them down on one side of the page.
3   Do your best to keep going until you reach the end of the page (this might mean thinking of about 25 words). And please do keep at it because, in my experience, the last five words usually contain something that is of fundamental importance to you and may well end up in your eventual top five core values.
4   If you're not very disciplined or find it hard to concentrate, ask a friend (or mentor if you're lucky enough to have one) to help drive your thought process or if you can afford it, pay a coach to help you.
5   Now study your list carefully and, assuming you can only have 10 of these important factors, eliminate the rest

(this part could take a while though it's absolutely worth the effort when it comes to your happiness and success at work). You'll need the rest of the page for scribbling on as it can be a messy process. If you're finding this tricky or messy or simply prefer an automated version, use the tool on my website which will give you an easier, more accurate result.

6   Once you get to 10, eliminate a further five (you'll still need these later).

7   Now put the remaining five in order of priority by importance.

These top five are your core values; the fundamental things you must have at work to remain enthused and able to progress. You'd be surprised how many people know 'things aren't quite right' at work though can't quite identify why – it's usually because although on the face of it, things are fine, underneath there is something that's in conflict with their personal values.

So it won't surprise you to know…
If one of your core values is 'achievement', you won't be able to thrive in an environment where people aren't focused on the goal and constantly fail to get things done.

If 'self-reliance' is a core personal value, being in a situation where people are micro-managed isn't going to work for you. If your core values include 'trust' yet there's a prevailing culture of 'guilty until proven innocent', you're on a road to nowhere…

Values 6-10 are still important, though, as these are your desired values; the ones you'll be prepared to compromise on.

So how do you use these values?
★   When you're job seeking, check out an organization's website – most list their values, though even if they don't, you should get a feel for what their culture is like.

★   Ask in your interview what their company values are –

TRUE STORY: THE POWER OF VALUES

James had enjoyed a stellar rise up the career ladder and was MD of a successful business by the time he was 26. Despite a great salary and profit-related bonus, enviable benefits and working with a fantastic, hand-picked team, he wasn't feeling fulfilled. He was so busy at work that it didn't really occur to him to take time out to think about himself and his future. If it had occurred to James, he probably would have thought it unnecessary because things always seemed to work out OK anyway. However, after a particularly frustrating meeting with his board, who yet again had turned down one of his proposals to expand the business, he was persuaded by a friend to work through the values exercise above. James was surprised to discover that his number one value was 'freedom'. He'd never really thought about it before; his frustration was about not having the freedom to progress his ideas; things he knew would make the company even more successful, yet were at odds with the risk-averse nature of his board. As a result, after a failed management buyout attempt, James walked away from the comfort, status and salary of his role, handed back his company car keys and started up on his own. He's never looked back.

---

    if they struggle to explain or laugh you out of the place, that
    should tell you something.

★   Or if you don't feel comfortable using the 'V' word, ask
    your interviewer what's important to their company about
    the way business is done. If they don't have an answer, that
    should tell you something too.

★   And if you feel you aren't able to ask the interviewer
    directly (or for some reason, it's not appropriate – more
    about that in Chapter 13), find a way to chat to the
    receptionist and/or others to see what they feel the
    company is all about.

★   And of course being true to yourself is a cracking way to
    be happy at work so make sure the work you do and where
    you do it is always aligned with your own values. You can
    compromise for a while, but sustained conflict will burn
    you out/make you ill/depressed/unhappy.

IF YOU ONLY DO THREE THINGS:

1 Spend some 'me time' thinking this through
   – it's good for your health.
2 Define your top five personal values ASAP and use them.
3 Do this exercise every year or two because your priorities
   will change as you progress.

ONE OF OUR RECRUITS **LEARNED OUR VALUES BEFORE HE CAME FOR INTERVIEW AND TALKED TO US ABOUT THEM –** I WAS IMPRESSED, I CAN TELL YOU. HE'S STILL WITH MY COMPANY AND GUESS WHAT,

HE'S OUR **VALUES MENTOR.**

| **05** | SO **WHAT** DO YOU WANT TO DO AND **WHERE** DO YOU WANT TO DO IT?

When you're small, you are often asked 'What do you want to do when you grow up?' Sadly, many 30-somethings are still puzzling over that very question. There are some rare people (like lucky old Mia in Chapter 3) who have an unshakeable belief in what they want to become. That's great; half the battle is knowing what you want to focus on.

What if you really don't know? Aside from careers advice during education, there are things you can do throughout your career superhighway to find out what might ultimately enable you to be happy and successful.

Having worked on your values, you will have a few ideas about what you don't want to do. However, it's vitally important that you are working towards something and not away from something else. I meet lots of people who are very definite about what they don't want though don't have much idea about what they do. People who are operating with an 'away from motivation' rarely end up making the right decisions and sometimes even end up worse off. If you are constantly moving away from something, think about what it is you want to change and what would instead give you what you want.

A **TRUE** STORY:

Fran didn't want to work in an open plan office because she kept being interrupted and found the surrounding noise made it difficult to concentrate on detailed parts of her work. An opportunity arose to take a role where she could work from home. Living alone, this gave her ample quiet, uninterrupted work time and she found she became far more productive. However, after a short while she found that she missed working in a team, she missed seeing people every day and just having them around. Eventually she began to lose focus and became unhappy. When Fran thought about what she did want and what was important to her, she discovered that being part of a team and being social were as significant as getting her work done in peace. She began to think about changing career altogether…

Fast forward and Fran is back working in an open plan office, in a similar role. She's happy, productive, motivated. The difference is she's in an organization where there is respect for personal space. If Fran and her new colleagues don't want to be disturbed, there are little flags they can raise on the top of their computers so people know not to interrupt. People are encouraged to wear earphones if they want to block out background noise and chatter, home working is permitted, and there are social events and team meetings where Fran can get her people fix.

Fran's story illustrates the importance of towards motivation and considering all desired outcomes in order to find the right role. It also demonstrates the importance of culture and environment. So as well as thinking about what you want to do, think about where you want to do it.

WHAT DO YOU WANT TO DO?

- Think about the type of roles andd/or organizations that might meet your core and desired values.
- Research these roles and environments on the internet.
- Talk to people you admire. If you don't know anyone personally, think about someone you've come across who is in a role you might be interested in. This might be a local businessperson, or someone you read about or spotted on a business-networking site. Be brave and drop them an email. Most successful people didn't get there by being horrible and so they may well respond to your request for advice (there's a great story about Richard Branson giving entrepreneurial advice to a 12 year old – that's Sir Richard Branson; billionaire owner of the

Virgin Group…). Keep it short, snappy and specific, thank them in advance and say something positive about their achievements (though avoid going over the top, being over-familiar or cheesy).

- **O** Think about all of the people in your social networks (virtual and otherwise), look at professional networks like 'LinkedIn', alumni networks, trade networks and so on…

- **O** Think about who knows who, family members' contacts, and their contacts. If you consider this, you probably have a massive web of people who you can speak to – you just need to do some detective work.

- **O** My mum used to say "it's not what you know it's who you know". I'd update that to "it's not who you know but who they know".

- **O** Above all, take responsibility; if you get a lucky break then great, though most people have to help the luck along. And remember that old cliché; if you don't ask, you won't get.

- **O** Get as much work experience as you can – see Chapter 6. If you're already in a role, this probably means looking for opportunities to develop the skills you'll need for the next one (even if this involves extra work).

WHERE DO YOU WANT TO DO IT?

The business environment consists of factors that you, the individual, are unlikely to be able to control. It therefore follows that working in the right type of environment is very important when it comes to being happy and successful on a sustainable basis. So you'll need to aim for a place of work that fits with your values, character and aspirations.

Think about the type of workplace environment you're most likely to thrive in. Although the business world is constantly evolving, there are some constants to take into account. There are internal (micro) factors such as culture, size and remit and external (macro) such as economy, geographical and political factors.

There are many considerations such as corporate, small-medium employer or enterprise (SME), public sector, not-for-profit, ethical, traditional, innovative, entrepreneurial, service, product, risk-taking, risk-averse…

The easiest way to decide is to imagine how you would like things to be and then compare this with the options. You'll know by now that this book is a lot about thinking – please don't let this put you off – your happiness deserves a bit of effort and reflection.

IF YOU ONLY DO **THREE THINGS:**

1 Believe you can and will find the right role in the right environment (even if you have to make some compromises along the way).

2 Always work with a 'towards' motivation.

3 Make connections; use any contacts you can (however tenuous).

| 06 | EXPERIENCE ALONG THE WAY

Whatever stage of your career you're at, you can add to your employability appeal and therefore ability to land a job you'll love, be happy and progress in by using the experiences you gather along the way.

View everything you do in the context of 'how could this be useful to me at work?' so when you attend interviews and/or present yourself you can illustrate what you're saying with experience.

As an employer, I'd always favour someone who could tell me what they could do for my business and how, in practical terms, to one who quoted a whole lot of theory. Nowadays, experience isn't always valued as much as it was by previous generations because it's possible to access anything you need to know literally at the touch of a few buttons. Suppose you decided to become a business advisor; you could learn all about business via the internet. However, if you'd never managed a company, you wouldn't have the practical knowledge and know-how to be able to give sound, practical advice. This might sound far-fetched but there are hoards of graduates out there looking for roles in consultancy right now. Learning from the resources available is a great thing. Though everyone can do just that, so there is a definite advantage to supplementing what you know and can access with some practical understanding and application.

Experience is vital when applying for jobs. Drawing from experience when advertising for a role, the vast majority of employers ask for experience in a similar field to the role they are advertising – some do this just to whittle down the number of applications received.

YOU CAN FIND EXPERIENCE EVERYWHERE

Rob, a maths graduate, took a summer job in a factory sticking labels on bottles. This was pretty mind-numbing work. However, he noticed how the permanent workers banded together as a team, bantered their way through the day and really made the most of a pretty grim and un-stimulating environment. They took pride in their work and thought of their job as not only a means to an end but also that people were going to enjoy the product they were making. He noticed how they set up little competitions between themselves to see who could label the most bottles or who had the fewest rejects. They made their own motivation in spite of the rather abrupt and disrespectful supervisor. They wanted the work and they did everything they could to make the best job they could. Rob learned more about team dynamics, self-motivation and optimism during that summer than any amount of theory could have provided. And when he started job seeking for real, he used this to show his understanding of how teams can work and how he would be able to fit in.

Even if you've been working for many years, it's important to continue to broaden your horizons by seeking out opportunities to experience new things, always thinking:

- What's the lesson here?
- What can I take from this?
- How can I apply it?

Some suggestions around how you can broaden your experience:

- VOLUNTEER:
  - ★ Charity shops – a great way to gain customer service experience and build verbal skills with different audiences.
  - ★ Reading with school children – tests your communication skills, tolerance and tenacity.
  - ★ Becoming the trustee of a charity – valuable board-level experience.
  - ★ Getting involved with a local youth club, community

project or group – organization, persuasion
and motivation.

★ Overseas projects – ingenuity, drive and persistence.
★ Sports or other coaching – focus, patience, planning.
★ Samaritans – train successful applicants in counselling
and other skills.

There are thousands of volunteering websites looking for people
to support their organizations and help make a difference to
somebody's life. And being a volunteer tells an employer you are
a) a nice person b) energetic and prepared to fill your time c) have
good people skills d) spirited and courageous. What's not to like?

○ PART-TIME WORK:
Working in entry level roles in hospitality or retail, in particular,
will grow many useful skills:

★ working under pressure
★ customer service
★ communication
★ teamwork
★ building stamina
★ reliability, punctuality, dependability
★ personal presentation
★ organizational skills
★ what's expected at work
★ how a retail/hospitality/other business works
★ practical aspects like cashing up or using a cash register,
even how to clean properly!

○ JOIN A GYM OR TAKE ON A SPORTING CHALLENGE:
★ Captain of the football team – leadership skills,
inspiration, motivation, organization.
★ Ironman/woman challenge – tenacity, determination,
focus, stamina.
★ Run a desired distance (5K, 10K, full marathon) –
resolve, drive, energy, strength of mind.
★ Gym – goal focus, willpower, personal pride.

○ PROJECT WORK:
  ★ A good way of preparing for your next role.
  ★ At work, offer to solve a business issue in your own time.
  ★ Ask for opportunities to be involved in that will stretch you.
  ★ Support other teams.
  ★ Generally make yourself useful and show you are enthusiastic about learning and doing well.

○ SELF-STUDY:
  ★ Learning a language or skill, even if it's non-work-related, shows your capacity for learning, desire for self-improvement, tenacity.
  ★ Extra brownie points for learning a work-related skill, especially if it's one that will help you – and the business – progress.
  ★ Enter awards – the process will provide a rich learning experience and if you win or are shortlisted, you will be building your profile.
  ★ Read, read, read – there are millions of great books out there, magazines, newspapers, internet resources

---

AN EMPLOYER INTERVIEWS two candidates. One has worked hard to put herself through a marketing diploma, the other is asking the company to fund her marketing diploma. Which one gets the job?

○ BECOME A MENTOR (see Chapter 14)
  AND/OR FIND YOURSELF A MENTOR
  ★ A great way to expand your skills and network.

○ TRAVEL
You'll have heard it said, but travel really does broaden the mind – you can gain experiences that can't be equalled anywhere else. Some of the gains:

★ bravery and self-reliance
★ personal adventure/out of comfort zone
★ experience of different cultures and new perspectives on ways of life
★ meet all sorts of people
★ overcome challenges
★ ability to focus, be organized and keep a clear head
★ maturity/acquire life skills.

Get the picture? This skill stuff is amazing when you think about it.

AN OBVIOUS (AND TRUE) EXAMPLE:

Jasmine spent her summer volunteering at an orphanage in Vietnam. Not only did she travel to a wonderful country and experience fantastic sights, meet a diverse range of people, eat great food, visit cities and beaches, she also made a life-changing contribution. She learned to be practical and efficient. She came to realize how fortunate she was personally, and never to take her lot in life for granted again. She also gained a host of practical skills as well as a crash course in emotional intelligence and resilience.

Emma spent her summer watching re-runs of *Desperate Housewives*, playing *The Sims*, tweeting various celebrities and cataloguing her nail varnish collection.

Which one is gaining the most skills to demonstrate when she starts job seeking?

Remember to be very aware of the skills you are accumulating and – this is so important – what they've added to your skill set. And even more importantly, how these skills can be translated into the workplace to benefit an employer. Work experience can also give you ideas to push you towards a career choice.

IF YOU ONLY DO **THREE THINGS:**

1 Start building up your skills bank today (and think about stuff you've acquired already).

2 Work out how this could benefit a prospective role or employer (if you don't tell them, they won't know).

3 Use these skills attributes and experiences to create competitive advantage for yourself – whatever stage you're at in the career cycle.

| 07 | CHANGING JOBS AND MAKING THOSE **ALL-IMPORTANT DECISIONS**

It's virtually impossible to plan your career road because there are so many factors that you won't be able to influence. Impact those you can and be prepared to view everything else as an opportunity. If you've found yourself in a redundancy or other potentially negative situation, it might seem inconceivable to view it as an opportunity. However, there are thousands of people who have found themselves in an undesirable career situation and then ended up in a much better place. Staying positive needs a lot of effort, discipline and resolve. Ask someone you trust to help you. Where would Wimbledon tennis champion Andy Murray be without the faith and support of his team and fans?

Even if you can't plan the journey, it's important to have an idea of the destination: where in your life you want to be in three, five, or even 10 years. This is called a life plan and it's a really good idea to review this every year, perhaps on 1 January, in readiness for the year ahead.

USEFUL CLICHÉ: You can't influence what happens, but you can choose how you react to it.

Having proper goals that contribute to where you want to get to really works. Think about starting a journey into town and then jumping on any bus regardless of its destination, only to find yourself fed up and disappointed when you end up by the landfill site on the other side of the city.

It makes sense to check that the 'bus' you board is going in the right direction. Be realistic in your expectations; you might go a few stops on one bus and then jump onto another. You might even have to go back a few stops and start over. That's life.

Take your life journey in smaller manageable chunks and
be prepared to change route if you need to; as long as this
makes sense.

On your way into town, on this hypothetical bus, you might
stop off to have coffee with a friend who suggests a different
route and then continue your journey – it's the same in life.

From time to time you'll find yourself with a tricky decision to
make. As an example, you might be completely determined to
have a corporate sales career and then an opportunity arises
to help a friend start up his new business. This could give you
valuable business and entrepreneurial skills. It might also take
you off track. How do you decide whether to give it a go or
stick to 'Plan A'? People are faced with these types of dilemma
throughout their lives so – and listen up, this is really important
– YOU will need to learn how to make the decisions.

TEN TOP TIPS FOR DECISION MAKING:

1   Even worse than making the wrong decision is not to make
    one at all (procrastination really is the thief of time). Sad
    fact: you'll be long dead, so resolve now to do what you can
    to make every minute of your life count.

2   If you make a decision that doesn't work out then
    you will have progressed and learned something and
    can then adjust accordingly – preserve and develop this
    positive mindset.

3   Be prepared, and 'train' yourself, to be OK when you're
    outside your comfort zone – this is how people learn
    and progress.

4   Learn to think for yourself rather than asking 10 people's
    opinions and ending up even more confused (this is VERY
    common) – they are not you!

5   Take note of your 'gut feel', it's often right (though, sadly,
    not infallible).

6   If you need help thinking things through, find one trusted

friend or mentor who will ask you the right questions so as to help you think and decide rather than telling you what to do – they are not you either!

7 Take a blank page (paper or virtual). Make two columns. Head the first 'Pros' and the second 'Cons'. Then think really hard about all the reasons for and against the choice you might (or might not) make and note them down in the appropriate column. This simple technique will help crystallize your thoughts and will support you in thinking through options and alternatives, bringing clarity to the fore.

8 Ask yourself "If I take this choice, what's the worst thing that can happen?" You'll find that most decisions don't involve anything life threatening or truly dangerous and on that basis it will be possible to manage through the outcome, even if it turns out not to be the one you were expecting.

9 Think about your dilemma last thing at night as you drift off to sleep – with a bit of luck you might 'dream' the solution because this, and the time when you're waking, are your most creative times. If this backfires and keeps you awake, spend the time doing tip (7).

10 Be brave, find your 'inner cheerleaders' and let them give you more confidence and resolve:

GO YOU! GO YOU! GO YOU!

People change jobs for numerous different reasons; sometimes it's because they want to progress; other times because they're not happy where they are.

A **TRUE STORY:**

Grace felt miserable in her role. She really liked the company she worked for and the way they did things, and the money was pretty good. However, she just couldn't feel motivated or positive about her role and began to dread coming into the office each day. Soon her performance began to suffer and this led to more and more negative feedback from her manager and colleagues. She couldn't work out why she felt so miserable but was really worried about finding something else and feeling the same so she stuck it out. Her manager was on the point of starting a formal disciplinary process when a director asked Grace into his office for an informal chat. The director explained that he just wanted to help, knowing that it's impossible to perform well when so clearly unhappy. Instead of admonishing the non-conformances and drilling down into the detail, what happened next was a very empathetic, adult-to-adult conversation, at the end of which Grace said:

"I think I've made a massive mistake, I love the company and all you stand for, it's just the work that's wrong for me. I've thought about whether there's another role here for me but there just isn't. And I feel bad because I don't want to let people down. I'm so relieved we're talking like this."

As a result, they helped Grace to find her perfect job elsewhere. Everyone was happy with the outcome and the unpleasant, disruptive nature of formal performance management was completely avoided. By bringing the issue into the open and facing facts that things were never going to improve, Grace was able to move out of her 'comfort zone' and move on (she is still very happy in her new environment several years later).

IF YOU ONLY DO **THREE THINGS:**

1 Learn to stay positive; channel your 'inner cheerleaders'.
2 Work through the options and their pros and cons.
3 Once you start to feel it's time to move on, talk to your manager or mentor.

| **08** | THE **DEPARTURE LOUNGE**

So your decision is to move on. First make sure this is the right one; have you explored all the optional alternatives? If you're leaving because you're not happy, have you given the right people an opportunity to put things right?

Think about what you'll do if your employer makes you a counter-offer. What would it take to keep you here? What are the pros and cons of each role? It might be better to think about how you can improve your circumstances here rather than giving up altogether. My mum used to say: "The grass is always greener on the other side of the hill".

If you're thinking of leaving without a job to go to, be sure to work out your finances and how long you can manage without an income. It could take three to six months to find the right new role. Being miserable at work might, in the short term, be preferable to being poor and miserable out of work.

GIVING NOTICE:

Check how much notice you'll need to give – this should be in your contract, assuming you have one. If not, then do what's reasonable – even though you don't have to.

Please don't ever just walk out. If you do you will:
- let down colleagues and the organization
- leave the door firmly closed behind you
- tarnish your reputation (news travels – fast)
- show that you are unable to control your emotions or make sound, rational decisions
- be unlikely to receive a good reference (on or off the record).

And, anyway, it's just not the way to do things. However, you are entitled to leave without notice if you have been sexually harassed, are expected to do something unethical or illegal, if your physical or mental health is in danger or if you've not been paid for your work as agreed. Even in these circumstances, I'd hope you would raise it with someone in authority first.

If you are resolved to leave, please don't resign by email or by leaving a letter on your manager's desk for them to find when they return from their nice relaxing holiday in the Maldives. Man up. Have a meeting to explain the situation or at the very minimum give them a call. Be gracious, thanking them and the company for the opportunities they've given you. And certainly don't brag about your new role.

You will need to follow up in writing. Do this graciously and say thank you for the good bits. Keep it light and factual; resisting the urge to say why you are leaving. Avoid all negativity. Here's an example:

Dear Fred

This is to confirm my resignation from my position as IT developer here at Any co. As per my contractual notice, my last day will be 31 October.

I've really enjoyed my time here and would like to thank you for the many opportunities for professional and personal development that you have provided during the last three years. I really appreciate the support and encouragement you have given me and I hope we can stay in touch.

If I can be of any help during the transition or beyond, please let me know.

Yours

Julie

It is very important to leave every door open if you can and to remain honourable and polite throughout. The world is a very small place, news travels fast, and it's crazy to do anything that could ultimately damage your reputation. The colleague you fell out with yesterday might turn up as your manager tomorrow. So make style and grace your mantra for a smooth departure.

Be helpful, offer to train your replacement, write an induction plan and/or a guide to your role. You might wonder why you should bother – see above re. small worlds and being gracious and grateful for the good times. If you are unable to recall the good times, just think about all the money you've earned. And all the stuff you've learned (observing 'how not to' can provide some excellent development).

Never, ever write about your huge dislike and disrespect for the company and manager you are leaving. Unless you are Greg Smith of course, who famously slated his employer in *The New York Times* and landed a $1.5m book deal as a result. This is very unusual.

Bragging to colleagues achieves nothing, other than to cause people to regard you as immature, disruptive and unpleasant. Parking your brand new company BMW outside your old place of work serves no purpose other than to categorize you as a bit of a twit.

A **TRUE STORY:**

Amir, a successful sales manager, was offered a new role by a competitor company. He accepted this role and then handed in his resignation. His current employer then offered him more money, a company car and a bigger role. So he stayed put, letting his potential new employer down. Six months later he resigned from the new position and joined another company. Why?

COUNTER OFFERS:

What often happens when someone gives in their notice
is that their employer offers to improve their pay in order
to retain them. There is plenty of research which concludes
that money comes way down on the list of top motivators.

TOP FIVE MOTIVATORS AT WORK:

1 Communication/consultation

2 Good leadership/vision

3 Culture/value alignment

4 Development/progress

5 Career path/contribution

Source: Purple Cubed

Incidentally, in this piece of research, money appears at number
nine on the list.

Offering an increased package sometimes works in
the short term, but it is the equivalent of a sticking plaster
in that it papers over a few cracks temporarily yet the
underlying issues are still simmering away underneath. Giving
notice is a big decision, rarely taken lightly. Once the emotional
decision to leave has been taken, it is very difficult to get back
to a happy and satisfied place. People who stay due to financial
enticements often leave within the year. This shows the short-
term effect of finance as a motivator. Think very carefully before
being seduced away from your decision…

Amir's original reasons for looking for an alternative post were
to do with:

- lack of communication from his boss
- old-fashioned culture
- unwilling to invest in progressing the business/
  cost-cutting mentality
- a broad remit with little budget to be able
  to make a difference.

Even though Amir was given a bigger challenge and more money, even a company car, these short-term motivators could not compensate for the enormity of cultural mismatch and frustration at not being able to introduce more modern ways of working to propel the company forward.

So some points to consider if you find yourself in a counter-offer situation:

Control the emotion: it might be flattering and it's easy to get carried away by that. However, keep grounded and ask yourself why the offer is being made. Is it that you're so fantastic that you can't be replaced (it's a sad fact that everyone can – even the Queen of England has a successor or two in waiting)? Or is it merely that the inconvenience and expense of replacing you is far less attractive than offering you more money/a new title/a car?

Also under the emotional header comes guilt. You might be made to feel guilty that you are letting people down (or you might self-impose this guilt upon yourself). Don't do it – it is highly likely that you have contributed in equal, if not higher measure, to the investment made in you by your company.

If you do accept a counter-offer, remember that the trust of your colleagues and leadership team will probably have been damaged. Relationships might never be 'quite the same'. In an organization where loyalty is key, it might be impossible to function as before. Often this is the factor that ultimately drives the eventual departure.

Keep your own goals in sight – avoid being seduced by monetary gain if that's not your priority. Remember why it was that you were leaving in the first place. Will the new offer fix what needs to be fixed?

Retain control and remain professional.

HOUSEKEEPING –
PRACTICAL STUFF TO DO BEFORE YOU GO:

1 Clean up your PC: remove personal emails and files, make sure everything that remains is easily retrievable.
2 Leave your contact details and offer your support after you've moved on if they need it.
3 Work out your entitlements – you might be able to take your remaining holiday and finish earlier, for example.
4 Return all company property before you're asked for it
5 Email round a positive goodbye message to your colleagues – including something about what you've learnt during your time working with them.
6 Check how your employer wants to deal with telling your customers if applicable and handle this accordingly.
7 Ask for a written reference. Many organizations have a policy not to provide open references i.e. those 'To whom it may concern' ones that you can take away with you and show to anyone, though it's worth a try. They will probably respond to individual reference requests from a prospective new employer, however.

In an ideal world, your employer will arrange some sort of farewell for you. If not and you want to say goodbye to colleagues, then arrange an appropriate informal event. If you just can't face it, then bow out gracefully. Thanks for the memories…

3

IF YOU ONLY DO **THREE THINGS:**

1 Make sure you're leaving for the right reasons.
2 Be grown up, stylish and diplomatic.
3 Leave the door open with everyone thinking you're a great person.

MAKING IT **HAPPEN:**

| **09** | YOUR **CV**

So you've decided to make the move or seek an alternative role within your current company; what next?

The best way to secure an interview is through your network and/or a recommendation, which is why it makes sense to expand this as widely as possible, and as early into your career as possible. If you were considering buying a certain new mobile phone, you'd probably wantto know what friends and others thought about it. If you shop on Amazon, Trip Advisor, eBay there are always customer reviews to help people make their purchasing decisions.

If you think about it, for an employer, buying a book, new phone or even a holiday is far less risky than employing an unknown quantity; someone who is going to be responsible for important aspects of their business and be representing them to the public.

I'm sad to say it's generally the privileged few who are able to find their jobs through recommendations. Therefore, it's necessary to shorten the odds of success by giving the employer some comfort that you can perform. It's necessary to remove some of the guess-work. To do this your CV will need to illustrate exactly what you will do for the organization should you get the job.

Curriculum vitae (CV) is a Latin phrase which can be translated as 'the course of my life'. A CV is a summary (note the word summary) of a person's career achievements, qualifications and other relevant information (note the word relevant).

Put yourself in the employer's shoes. Which one of the CVs on the following pages would interest you more?

And why? Because CV2 looks less risky and really illustrates what the applicant is likely to achieve for you, the employer and your business. CV1 is bland, bland, bland – it does nothing to stand out from the crowd.

Lose the waffly paragraph at the beginning of your CV. It is far, far more effective to send a well-crafted email or letter along with an achievement-focused CV than to put the employer off with a boring diatribe about your supposed, non-evidence-based list of personal attributes. Your well-intentioned careers advisor probably spent ages helping you to write said paragraph. However, if you ask any employer they'll tell you they just don't have time to read the same stuff over and over again – it's offputting and an insult to their intelligence. Of course you're ambitious, organized, honest, numerate, computer literate, good at customer care, a skilled communicator… who's ever going to say they're not?

Name: Amber Itious
Address: 39 Street Road, London SW12 8EP
Tel: 0777 292 7198 | Email: amber.itious@btinternet.com

Personal profile:

I am a highly competent and experienced manager with a proven track record. I love the hotel industry and so am an excellent motivator and one who leads by example. I am organized and focused on the job in hand. I enjoy working with people and dealing with customers. I have strong financial acumen and a good all-round knowledge of the hotel business. I am very ambitious and hope that one day I will run my own hotel company.

Education:

1990 – 1994 Manchester Metropolitan University
BA (Hons) Hospitality Business Management (2:1)
1998 – 1990 Nettleford College of Technology
BTEC National Diploma in Hotel, Catering & Institutional Management
1984 – 1988 Bridgeport High School
10 GCSE passes – Grades A & B including A English and Maths

Employment history:

2006 – Present, Palms Hotel, Hawaii, General Manager

- Responsible for a 200-bedroom hotel, bar, restaurant, brasserie and meeting rooms
- Managed all services successfully over a period of six years
- Increased results against budget year on year
- Employed a happy, productive team
- Contributed to food and beverage culture within the hotel
- Worked on new Beach Bar concept
- Recognized in the group company awards as 'GM of the Year 2010/11'
- Awarded an accolade for leading, inspiring and supporting my team

2004 – 2006, Palms Hotel, Tahiti, General Manager

- Opened 64-bedroom hotel which went well and above expectations
- Financial results were above expectations
- Employed and managed 49 staff

2002 – 2004, Lake Hotels, Glasgow, General Manager

1997 – 2002, Lake Hotels, Manchester, Operations Manager

Have held various hospitality roles within the Holiday Inn, Crowne Plaza Manchester, Regents Park Hilton and Principal Hotel Group.

Hobbies:

Reading, cooking, keeping fit, collecting 'do not disturb' signs

CV | 2 |

Name: Amber Itious | **Address:** 39 Street Road, London SW12 8EP
Tel: 0777 292 7198 | Email: amber.itious@btinternet.com

Career highlights to date:

2006 – Present, Palms Hotel, Hawaii, General Manager
- Consistently exceeded budget in this 200-bedroom hotel, bar, restaurant, brasserie and meeting rooms
- Annual turnover - £12m – grew year on year by 20%+ over five years
- Increased budgeted EBITDA by 12%
- Achieved a growth of $20.55 on ARR and grew RevPar 6%
- Highest ranking for 'employee engagement' within group of 46 hotels in 2012
- Instrumental in developing and enhancing new food and beverage culture within the hotel – covers per week increased by more than double, average spend per head up 30%+
- Initiated and implemented successful Beach Bar concept – since rolled out group-wide
- Flagship property used as an introduction to the 'Palms Brand' for new recruits at senior level
- Recognized in the group company awards as 'GM of the Year 2010/11'
- Awarded the 'Most Supportive Manager' Leadership Foundation accolade in 2009.

2004 – 2006, Palms Hotel, Tahiti, General Manager
- Opened 64-bedroom hotel, recruited team, set brand standards in place and established venue as the leading lifestyle hotel in the region (Conde Naste Traveller).
- Exceeded projections with a year-one turnover year of £2.5m and EBITDA 15% in excess of projections.

2002 – 2004, Lake Hotels, Glasgow, General Manager
1997 – 2002, Lake Hotels, Manchester, Operations Manager
Have held various hospitality roles within the Holiday Inn, Crowne Plaza Manchester, Regents Park Hilton and Principal Hotel Group.

Education:
1990 – 1994 Manchester Metropolitan University
BA (Hons) Hospitality Business Management (2:1)
1998 – 1990 Nettleford College of Technology
BTEC National Diploma in Hotel, Catering & Institutional Management
1984 – 1988 Bridgeport High School
10 GCSE passes – Grades A & B including A English and Maths

Personal Achievements:
2011 London Marathon raising £15,000+ for The Variety Club Children's Charity
Walked 180 miles across The Great Glenway & West Highland Way to raise funds for Cancer Research contributing towards a £250K company target
Successfully completed the Executive Education Program at the Ecole Hoteliere Lausanne

TOP TIPS FOR TOP CVS:

1 Keep it factual.
2 Stress achievements/benefits and evidence them.
3 Use strong verbs like 'led', 'initiated', 'implemented', 'improved', 'enhanced', 'spearheaded'.
4 Keep it brief and well spaced, use bullets; people don't have time to read blocks of detailed text.
5 Keep to two pages maximum.
6 Use a modern-looking font.
7 Keep it neat and professional; the way you want to be perceived.
8 Allow your personality to shine through.
9 If a photo is requested (and it shouldn't be, so think about why they are asking) make sure you send a professional one (not you and your cat on holiday in Bognor).
10 Follow the format in CV2 above (or visit my website for a template).
11 Use experience from outside work as long as the related skills are relevant (see Chapter 6).
12 Leave out irrelevant trivia or that which could portray you negatively (it happens).
13 Omit referees' details as they can be sought later if required.
14 Number the pages i.e Page 1 of 2, Page 2 of 2 at the bottom and add your name to the bottom of page two in case pages are printed off and separated.
15 Make it easy for the employers to like you and want you on their team.

Here's an example of the sort of letter/email you could send to accompany your CV (you would need to tailor the language and style to the organization you're applying to – its website will help you):

Dear Katherine,

I was very excited to see that Roundhouse Hall has an opening for a Sales Executive. I am about to graduate from Randolf University and, having recently enjoyed a short internship at The Roundhouse Collection, I have a strong ambition to join your company. Based on my passion for hospitality, outgoing personality, creativity and excellent interpersonal skills, I am also looking to excel within Sales and Marketing. I therefore attach my CV.

I believe that my abilities, drive, ambition and personal presentation make me an ideal candidate for this opportunity. I am always the first to welcome a challenge, which I have proven many times when working both in retail and as a volunteer in our local Citizen's Advice Centre.

I have previous experience as a Sales and Marketing management trainee, where I have demonstrated that I have a flair for building and maintaining relationships with both clients and colleagues. I have also been in charge of social media management. Throughout my sales experience, my team sustained and exceeded corporate and leisure targets for our property through various sales initiatives.

I want to make a difference and am prepared to work hard; I am eager to learn, develop and grow within The Roundhouse Collection, and would love it if this position could become my first step on that pathway.

I really hope that I will have the opportunity to meet you soon.

Best Wishes

Felicity Bramwell

IF YOU ONLY DO **THREE THINGS:**

1 Overhaul your CV using the top tips.
2 Make it achievement-focused – with evidence ('sell' yourself)
3 Accompany it with a short, well-crafted email customized to the company and role on offer.

| **10** | HOW TO **APPLY**

If you are intending to apply for an internal move, the chances are the process is established and clear. Make sure you read the requirements carefully, respond fully in the requested way and add in some bonus 'selling points'. Do your homework – find out as much as you can about the role/department/team, seek out people who can help and advise you and use your networks.

YES – RESEARCH IS VITAL!

If applying elsewhere, exactly the same rules apply, though remember it's unlikely the prospective employer will have the same opportunity to 'check you out' as an internal one, so follow these guidelines:

- Search yourself on the internet and clean up anything that could portray you in a less than positive light. For example, if your Facebook profile picture shows you and a gang of topless girls on a podium in Malia, then it might be better to replace it with the one your mum took at Christmas. Also, if you're a tweeter, clean up your feed and impress the potential employer by tweeting about a couple of things which would be of relevance to their business.
- Look at the job ad – online or otherwise – what does it say about the company? Do they sell themselves to you? Can you get a handle on their culture? Here is one we use at my company:

MARKETING MANAGER
– JOIN THE PURPLE REVOLUTION

Recognised as an inspirational place to work, Purple Cubed is seeking an exceptional, client-focused person to join our growing business development team in London, UK. Over the past 12 years we've created one of the most innovative and exciting business transformation organisations in the UK. We help well-known brands across the world (think Hakkasan, Village Urban Lodges, Orient Express…), to improve company performance, people engagement and profit, helping them become great places to work.

If you're up for a challenge, would like to gain experience in a fast-paced business environment and are known for building strong client relationships, here's the deal:

- we'll give you freedom (within a framework); an exciting challenge and a chance to shine
- you'll help us grow the company
- we'll teach you about business and people
- you'll progress and develop towards your full potential
- we'll benefit from your considerable talents
- you'll be special: flexible, positive, self-sufficient, and enthusiastic.

Reporting to the Head of Commercial Development, you'll:

- deliver the marketing communications strategy using a range of innovative marketing techniques
- grow and enhance our social media presence
- develop new marketing tools for the promotion of our wide range of technology solutions
- organise a range of events for our new 'Clubs' concept
- lead PR for the business; writing new content and building strong relationships with key titles.

In return for working in one of the best environments anywhere, you'll:

- be polished, confident and service focused
- be organised, proactive and able to build rapport
- plus have the ability to take responsibility and get the job done without a fuss.

Email 10 bullet point reasons why you're the one, plus a one-page CV to **emily@purplecubed.com**

We look forward to hearing from you
Emily Moore - Head of People, Purple Cubed

- Research the company, person/people doing the selection and the role as much as you can. You won't need to use all of this info at interview (you don't want to come across as a stalker) though making it clear that you've done your homework will definitely impress the employer. Make sure that if you do this you get your facts right and understand what you're talking about though or you could end up worse off than if you hadn't bothered.
- Take note of the style of the organization's website – it will give you an idea about their culture. Check out its people pages – does it make applying easy and interesting? Does it create a compelling picture of itself as an employer?
- Ask your friends and networks what they know – by the law of the six degrees of separation (which, with social networks is now about four degrees) you can probably find someone who works there. In short; do your homework.
- Read the application form and take careful note of what they want you to do.
- Put yourself in the interviewers' shoes – what would impress you if you were them?

I love this recruitment campaign:

SAATCHI & SAATCHI X LONDON GRADUATE
'LIFT PITCH' RECRUITMENT CAMPAIGN:

Seeking "entrepreneurial, creative, 360° thinkers" so posed an online challenge
- 650 applicants posted video applications
- no form filling: 100 successful applicants invited to Saatchi & Saatchi X London offices to film a 'Lift pitch'
- basis of this – are lifts awkward or an opportunity? Grads were asked to imagine they had met Saatchi & Saatchi X London executives in an elevator and had 30 seconds to impress
- leadership team interviewed 100 people in one day
- all grads had a fun and creative learning experience
- top 40 interviewed more formally

- final 17 sent to boot camp
- final two selected. See www.facebook.com/xliftpitch.

From the moment you make contact, you are 'on stage' selling yourself – think about all of the things you could do to make a fab first impression and keep building on that…

At Purple Cubed we ask for a one-page CV and 10 bullet points as our entire application process.

This tells the candidate something about our company. We:
- like to make things simple
- value creativity and originality
- are achievement-focused
- have high expectations and robust brand standards
- need people who can write persuasively in a succinct way
- want flexible people who are observant
- need those who can follow our ways of doing things and are prepared to make an effort.

About 90% of the people who apply completely ignore the specified application process and therefore are rejected. We also discard:
- applicants who can't count up to 10 and write a different number of points
- applications that present poorly or have spelling and grammatical errors
- people who write 'Dear Sir or Madam' instead of the named person
- people who don't bother to edit their CV down to one page.

As you can imagine, this means that we only ever interview about 5% of the people who apply to us. Sounds harsh? Not really – we're striving for a high performance culture.

Recruiting this way streamlines our process and also makes sure we don't waste the time of anyone who wouldn't be happy and successful within our company.

Oh, and we always offer feedback to unsuccessful applicants. Hardly anyone ever takes this up, though it's a golden opportunity for any applicant to improve next time. Accept any feedback you get gracefully; it's neither smart nor classy to have a big whine at anyone who's trying to help you improve.

So please take note and follow the instructions specified in the recruitment advert or other source.

If you're not successful, be resilient.

A **TRUE STORY:**

Kam was transitioning from a lucrative career in consultancy into a human resources role. She did her homework, put together a compelling application, sent off her information and waited. In just one day she received 20 rejections. She was feeling pretty bad though she knew she had to keep going and be resilient. She told herself "it's their loss". Things worked out in the end - it just takes a while sometimes.

IF YOU ONLY DO **THREE THINGS:**
1 Do your homework – get informed and stay strong.
2 Clean up your act – be the best 'you' you can be.
3 Follow the instructions specified to the letter (unless you are applying to a maverick organization where breaking all the rules is expected – this is highly unlikely; and even mavericks expect everyone else to do things their way).

| **11** | PREPPING FOR **INTERVIEWS**

You've managed to land yourself an interview. This is your opportunity to shine, to stand out from the crowd and land your dream job. Make sure you give yourself the best possible opportunity to succeed – leaving things to chance is not smart:

FROM THE METRO 'GOOD DEED FEED' SEPTEMBER 2013
"THANK YOU SO much to the man who helped me prepare for my first job interview on the train from Huddersfield. I couldn't have done it without you."

Put yourself in the shoes of the interviewer – if you were them what would you want to know? You can find some examples of interview questions in Chapter 20 – make sure you do some work on being prepared. Think about your responses to the stuff you might be asked. Practice your responses while looking in a mirror – how do you come across? Keep practising – especially if you're feeling nervous or apprehensive, if you 'know your stuff' it will really help and take away the fear of the unknown.

BIG IMPORTANT FACT:
INTERVIEWERS ARE ONLY PEOPLE.
THEY ARE NO BETTER
OR WORSE THAN YOU ARE.
THEY WERE ONCE IN YOUR POSITION AND
PROBABLY FELT AS UNSURE AS YOU DO.

The most important thing to remember is: be yourself. On that note you might want to make sure your privacy settings on any social media sites are OK so that if a prospective employer decides to search you on the internet, you don't come up on that podium in Malia.

A WHILE AGO I was interviewing graduates to join Purple Cubed. I asked one candidate what sort of things he did to let his hair down.

HE RESPONDED THUS: "I go to the library and hang out with my friends. I don't really go out much – especially during the week".
CONTRAST THIS WITH his Twitter feed from the evening before: "Staying in tonight – boring – have an interview in the morning so can't get wasted ☹"

When joining a new company or new department in your existing one, cultural fit is really important (see Chapter 4). You'll need to be able to relate and align with the values of the place you're joining. By being yourself, open and honest you'll both be able to get a good picture of how things could work between you. So if you're pretending to be 'library boy' and really you're 'party animal' that's not going to give a true reflection.

So when you're prepping for the interview, think about how your personality can shine through.

Many job seekers ask "But what if they don't like me?" Well that's fine, if you're not right for the role or organization then the role or organization is probably not right for you either, so congratulate yourself on having had a lucky escape and move on. You might need to kiss a few proverbial frogs before you discover the prince or princess of jobs.

Conversely, don't go to the other extreme and tell the interviewer everything about you. In the same round of interviews as mentioned above, one candidate went into great detail about her nervous breakdown and eating disorder. Of course we would never discriminate against someone who had been ill, though did knowing the gory details help this candidate present herself in a compelling light? Sometimes in a first interview, the old adage 'keep your own counsel' would be advisable so plan accordingly and decide how much you're going to disclose. By planning ahead you'll be more in control and won't let your chatty, open nature work against you.

Remember why you are attending the interview; plan accordingly so you can present yourself in the best light. As mentioned previously – do your homework. Find out everything you can about the organization and their culture, the role you are applying for and the person(s) who will be interviewing you. You don't need to relay all of this information in the session, but it will make you feel more confident and informed. As well as the company website, put the interviewer's name into a search engine and also check them out on LinkedIn and Twitter. If you can find something you have in common that will help you build rapport with this person – make sure you get your facts right though; if in doubt, don't use the information.

USEFUL CLICHE: ALWAYS

dress for the next job, not the one you're in now. Otherwise you could be missing an opportunity to impress. As a rule of thumb - match and mirror the best examples at the place you're going to.

Plan what you're going to wear and make sure it's ready, clean and pressed (see Chapter 12). Wear something you'll feel comfortable and confident in and always dress for the next role, not the one you're in or applying for now. And if you're unsure of the office dress code, take a look at the people section on their website (if there is one) and judge your outfit based on this; if in doubt always overdress – don't assume that because it's a creative role, jeans are appropriate attire. And this is not the time to try out a new pair of brogues or start experimenting with new make-up or unfamiliar clothing items.

COPING WITH NERVES:

Nerves are a good thing because they will help give your 'performance' an edge. Some of the best actors and actresses are sick with nerves before they go on to turn out an Oscar-winning performance. Do as they do and use your nerves to your advantage.

The feelings of nervousness are caused by stress hormones being released in the body to help you cope with the challenge ahead. They're there for a positive reason, so make a conscious decision now to embrace your nerves; harnessing them to work for you and not against. This is always going to be a work-in-progress; something you'll need to keep revisiting and working on to make it an asset, not an inhibitor. You really do have the power. Being prepared is a great weapon in the fight against negative feelings. As well as finding out all the information you need, look after yourself, be healthy, exercise, eat well. Get some sleep. Chill out. Be kind to yourself. And if nerves take hold, take lots of deep breaths until you feel calm.

TOP TIP: When nerves take hold, perspiration often flows. Avoid the 'wet-fish' handshake (which is instantly offputting) by practising a firm handshake beforehand. When you arrive, either visit the bathroom and wash your hands in cool water, drying thoroughly, or failing that wipe your hand surreptitiously on your trousers before going in for the shake.

Ask people for their interview stories. Imagine the interview going really well and keep thinking ahead to this positive scenario – visualizing a positive outcome will really help you to make it a reality. This is where a bit of mind control comes in very handy indeed.

IF YOU ONLY DO **THREE THINGS:**

1 Do your homework and prepare yourself for this challenge.
2 Work through potential questions and practise in the mirror.
3 Psych yourself up, breathe deeply and imagine things going really, really well.

12 | THE **GENERATION GAME** AND WHY IT MATTERS

At this point, it's important to introduce information that will help not just in the interview process, but throughout your entire career highway.

This is a key chapter because it will equip you with the essential knowledge to understand why different age generations can have varying points of view, which sometimes then results in conflict. It also provides you with the tools to help deal with this and engage people of a different generation to yourself. Use it well and this little chapter will save you a whole lot of hassle now and in the future. Generation theory is a subject that is sometimes contentious, yet there is plenty of evidence and research to back up the fact that it's well grounded and sound. However, it's important to remember that everyone is different (which should be applauded and celebrated). There are always exceptions to the rule, so test out your thoughts rather than making assumptions based on what you read here.

A SHORT TRUE TALE OF GEN X VS GEN Y:

15 year old daughter: "'It's my friend Will's birthday tomorrow."
Me: "That's nice, why don't you send him an e-card?"
Her: "Mum, what century are you in?!"

Generation theory seeks to explain how individuals born within one generation (approximately a 20-year period) will have a different view of the world to those born in another. This is because each generation is shaped by differing economic, environmental and social norms. Because of the advances in technology, this has speeded up and so it's widely thought that those born in the mid-90s (now termed Generation Z) are already different from their predecessors in Generation Y (those born in the 80s). What does that mean? Read on…

These generations see things differently because they have grown up with different influences. A simple, and perhaps extreme, example would be a baby boomer who grew up without TV and had to walk ten minutes to use the telephone in a public phone box versus a Gen Z with instant, high-speed access to a variety of media and connectivity in their hand.

So you can imagine how potential miscommunication, distrust and even conflict could occur in the workplace if these two individuals working alongside each other weren't able to come to understand and value each others' differences.

GENERATION	BORN BETWEEN	ALSO KNOWN AS	KEY INFLUENCES
Generation Z:	1995 – 2012	Internet generation Gen I Digital natives	High-speed internet, smartphones, unlimited, instant access to media/ all info
Generation Y:	1981 – 1994*	Millennials Echo boomers	Education, technology, parental input/support, terrorism, social networks
Generation X:	1962 – 1980	Lost generation Latchkey kids	Divorce rate, working parents/redundancies, crime rates, MTV, AIDS
Baby Boomers:	1945 – 1961	The Big Bulge The Joneses	Post-war years, human rights, freedom, rock 'n' roll, protests, travel

*The emergence of this new generation as a result of high-speed internet and its influences on a new generation alters the generally regarded dates of Gen Y and I have amended accordingly.

A word of caution: every generation will be influenced by later generations so it's not unusual to find, for example, a Boomer who views the world in a similar way to a Gen Y. That is great. This chapter is there for those who revert to type and endure conflict as a result.

There are various opinions about the exact dates for each generation, so I'll use the ones we ascribe to. Don't get too hung up on the dates though – it's the differences in attitudes and characteristics that are important.

These influencers will inevitably impact upon each person's 'map of the world'. This is why a Gen Y employee would expect flexibility, work-life balance and to have his or her views heard and respected whereas his Gen X line manager might well find these opinions unacceptable and alien. On the following page is a table detailing some of the likely characteristics of each generation. This highlights the need to be mindful of all generations and points of view, to treat people as individuals and for leaders to understand that the people they manage may well be very different from themselves. It's necessary to accept and embrace this rather than attempt to change what has been shaped from childhood by events, family and community. For the person who wants to be happy and successful at work, it's possible to use this knowledge to 'manage upwards'.

A **TRUE SCENARIO:**

Darren and Dan secured investment for an internet start-up company. Darren and Dan are in their late 40s; their new chairman, courtesy of the investor, is 26. They wear suits, he wears jeans and a T-shirt. They learn from each other; through compromise, understanding and tolerance; through questioning and listening they have been able to build a successful business. It could easily happen to you so embrace diversity and delight in change – the opposite is painful and doesn't go well for anyone.

If you're part of Gen Y or Z be mindful that the way you see the world is likely to be very different from that of your Boomer or Gen X boss. Be prepared to modify your approach in order to achieve the result you want.

BABY BOOMER	GEN X	GEN Y	GEN Z (MY PREDICTIONS)
Live to work	Work to live	Work to fund lifestyle	Live then work. Workplace irrelevant, new ways of working
Long hours and dedication	Do the necessary and go home	Work-life balance, bored easily	Flexible, rapid progress, achievement without accountability
Motivated by prestige, perks, status	Motivated by change, freedom, respect, outputs	Motivated by making a difference	Motivated by being heard, progress, change
Knowledge = Power	'Show me what you know'	Ask many questions (Generation 'Why?')	Find own answers and offer solutions, value brands
Compliance, parent-child relationship with employer	Adult-to-adult relationships	Confidence to have adult-to-adult relationship	Offer opinions (often to the CEO); equality the norm
Know they've done a good job	Like regular feedback	Like immediate feedback	Constant feedback from variety of sources
Make own decisions without consultation	Take direction and then get on with it	Need constant collaboration/ direction	Need consultative approach, listen and be listened to as individual
Like structure and hierarchy	Have disdain for authority and structure	Family values – require nurturing environment	Secure and loved, parental support, expect same at work
Like control	Hate being micro-managed	Need help with problem solving, like to share	Find info rather than thinking it through, expect top technology
Want to lead	Self-reliant, cynical	Don't want to lead	Don't like hierarchy,
Resist change	Relish change	Flexibility	Super-flexible, diversity the norm

BABY BOOMER	GEN X	GEN Y	GEN Z (MY PREDICTIONS)
Value experience	Assert individuality	Experience irrelevant	Creative use of technology to find out anything/everything
Competitive and resilient	Want to fix Boomers' 'mistakes'	Take on tough, meaningful jobs	Manage outputs not inputs; want to do it their way
Parents said "You can do anything"	"Stand on your own two feet"	"You're wonderful and brilliant at everything"	"You can be anything you want to be; whatever you do is OK with us"
Kept opinions to themselves	Shared their opinions	Think you want to know their opinions	Know you need to know their opinions
Write to me	Meet me	Conference call/Skype me	Whatsapp me/Facetime

If you're a Boomer or Gen X employee working for a Gen Y boss, there's much to be gained and enjoyed from a new approach, so learn, be prepared to adapt and go with it.

IF YOU ONLY DO **THREE THINGS:**

1. Embrace diversity and be prepared to compromise.
2. Ask the right questions and learn to understand people's point of view.
3. Learn to accept and celebrate that that the ways things used to be are different to the way things are now (and will be in the future).

13 | BEING **THE BEST 'YOU'** YOU CAN BE

The sooner you get your head around this concept and resolve to make it a lifelong work-in-progress, the closer you will be to becoming successful and happy at work. Start with the premise that everyone can be just that little bit better every day. If you were to make just a 1% improvement each day, within a little over three months you'd be 100% better than you are now. While that's easier written than done, if you don't aim high, you're unlikely to see the improvements you're imminently capable of. And what's 'better'? Well, only you know that.

An easy way to improve is by doing something you love. Enjoying whatever it is that you spend your day doing gives an easy leg-up to motivation and energy. If you're not enjoying what you do, think about how you can change it.

A **TRUE STORY:**

Craig was pressured into a career in law by overzealous careers advisors and demanding parents. Having secured a first-class law degree, he climbed the ladder into one of the big four London law firms, eventually making partner and a six-figure salary. Married and with two children, his massive work-load meant that he barely saw them, holidays were cut short, weekends often consisted of working in the study. He was bored, exhausted, unfulfilled and stressed out. For the last 20 years, Craig has talked privately about his unhappiness at work and his dream to enter the wine business – to date he never has…

There are millions of people toiling away in jobs they hate for the wrong reasons. It's hard to improve and feel motivated to push the limits if you're not doing something you can relish. Sometimes people make sacrifices for their family or others – this is selfless and noble but not always smart. Use this as an absolute last resort and be creative about finding ways to 'have it all'.

USEFUL CLICHE: LIFE is not a rehearsal...

FROM THE LONDON METRO 'SEND US YOUR TEXT':
"IS IT JUST me or is there anyone else out there who hates their job but has no idea what else to do? Suggestions please"
Clare, Birmingham

So the first step to being the best 'you' you can be is to be true to yourself and make sure you're doing what you're doing for you and not to please everyone else. Billionaire author J.K. Rowling went from poverty and failure to massive success only when she took the decision to pursue her dream and devote her time to writing her Harry Potter books. Making this shift can be hard, particularly if you're young and under parental/other influences, or when you have commitments such as a mortgage and a family to think about. Three things you could do are:

1 Find a mentor who will advise and cheer you on from the sidelines.
2 Take changes in small steps or manageable chunks, rather than making radical ones.
3 Have faith that pursuing what you know you're really good at will work out if you put enough effort in.

PLEASE REMEMBER THAT YOU ARE VERY UNLIKELY TO BE ABLE TO FIND HAPPINESS AND FULFILMENT AT WORK IF YOU'RE DOING SOMETHING YOU DON'T LIKE. PEOPLE WILL ALSO KNOW...

KNOW WHAT YOU WANT. This is important because, as with any goal, you need to plan how to get there. If you don't know, how do you decide which route to take? Only by thinking

---

TIME OUT MAGAZINE, NOVEMBER 2013:
"**I CAN TASTE** how much you hate your job in my coffee. Can I have a fresh one with some love in it please?"

'big picture' can you nurture your talent and review your vision every day, ensuring you make progress.

Suppose you dream of being a catwalk model. Let's be realistic, it's highly unlikely that you'll be scouted à la Campbell or Moss. So instead of trusting chance and fate, work out whether you have what it takes – ask professionals who work in that arena. Obviously your mum or your best friend will tell you that you have the 'X factor' so go ask someone who is dispassionate. If you still believe you have the required attributes, work out the steps you'll have to take to get yourself there. I know a few teenagers who have such a belief they'll be discovered that they didn't bother to pursue other routes to success such as qualifications, careers advice and work experience. Instead they spend their time outside fashion stores along Oxford Street. This is a bad decision – even Lily Cole got herself into Cambridge University.

BELIEF is important and if you're really determined, as long as you're not in pursuit of the impossible, it's likely you'll get there. It's good to dream, but a touch of realism can help to avoid disappointment along the way.

LOOKING THE PART. The saying goes 'dress for your next job, not the one you're in'. By making the absolute best of yourself in the context of the position you want to inhabit, you will feel the part and people will regard you as such. There's no excuse for lapsing off – always be the best you can be – you owe it to yourself. If you don't know how to look the part, find out by researching on the internet or asking an appropriately attired person you admire. Or book a session with a professional image advisor – always money well spent.

TAKE A RISK. By staying totally safe and risk-free, it's unlikely you'll be able to kick-start the changes that need to be made to propel yourself forward. Make sure your risks are calculated ones though – listing the 'pros and cons' is an excellent place to start. And always ask yourself "If I pursue this course of action, what's the worst that could happen?"

> **USEFUL CLICHE:** WHAT DOESN'T KILL you only makes you stronger.

LEARN TO DEAL WITH FAILURE. Some failure is probably inevitable unless you live your life with so much caution that you find you haven't really lived at all – in which case you'll fail by default. It's a good thing – a great way to learn and find out how not to do something. So live a little – you might just enjoy it. Welcome mistakes as learning experiences and opportunities to toughen up and become more resilient.

ROLE MODELS. Observe others who are 'the best' – find out how they got there. You can probably do this from afar (avoid stalker syndrome) though perhaps you could persuade them to meet to answer your questions. Go to places they go so you can run into them. You might even be able to tempt them or someone they know into becoming your mentor (see Chapter 14).

CLEAR THE CLUTTER. Becoming the best 'you' will be significantly easier if you're organized. So clear the clutter – it'll not only make you feel good, you really will be able to 'see the wood for the trees'.

BE KIND TO YOURSELF. In the same way that small children need encouragement and nurturing to thrive, it makes sense to nurture and reward yourself for minor successes. Give yourself praise and recognition – that way you won't need to rely on others to do it.

JUST DO IT. In the words of 'Nike'. Take action; pontificating, prevaricating and procrastinating will get you nowhere.
Be brave, dive in, the water's lovely…

As American poet Maya Angelou once said: "Nothing will work unless you do".

IF YOU ONLY DO **THREE THINGS:**

1 Resolve now to be the best 'you' you can be and write down what that 'looks like'.
2 Do something every day to improve yourself in some way.
3 Be brave, laugh at and learn from the failures and celebrate the achievements.

14 | THE **POWER** OF MENTORING

Mentoring is nothing new. If you're into mythology or just like a good tale, you'll be interested to know that the term originated from Homer's Odyssey. The story goes that whilst Odysseus, King of Ithaca, is away fighting the Trojan war, he entrusts the care of his household to Mentor, in particular the education and guidance of his son, Telemachus. After the war (10 years later), Odysseus is condemned to wander in an attempt to return to Ithaca. Telemachus, who by now has grown up, sets out to find his father and also wanders. At this point good old Athena, Goddess of War, turns up, assumes the form of Mentor (who by now is an old man) and guides Telemachus on his troubled quest. Father and son are reunited (hurrah), reclaiming Odysseus' throne and Telemachus' birthright.

Hit Google and you'll find numerous definitions of what mentoring is. To keep things simple, mentoring is where one person with more experience, knowledge or specialist expertise guides another. It's not so much about occasional advice but a relationship, which builds over time (either ongoing or for a set period). Ideally both parties will learn from one another.

It is very important that if you're going to be a mentor or find a mentor, you know what you're doing, otherwise you could waste a lot of time and/or fail to achieve a healthy, productive and mutually beneficial relationship.

You might use different mentors at different times. For example, when starting in a new role you might have a buddy mentor to help you settle in and learn the ropes. You might be on a fast-track leadership programme and be mentored by a more senior leader. You might join a formal internal or external mentoring programme. Some universities have student/employer mentoring schemes which are very mutually beneficial (in fact I'd urge every university to implement this). You might look for someone to help you on the next step; be it changing role, starting something new or just to assist you with a particular project or challenge.

The important thing is to think hard about why you would like a mentor and the specifics of what you'd like them to help you with. Start with the goal in mind. There's little point flitting around collecting mentors and not really having an agenda.

A mentor should NOT:
- do your job for you
- do your thinking for you
- manage you
- make all the decisions
- set the agenda
- set your goals
- talk more than listen
- have all the answers
- be the Oracle of Delphi
- be shy about giving honest, constructive feedback
- be judgemental or superior in approach
- be your coach*
- be a preachy know-all
- assume things are the same now as they were 'in their day'
- become your saviour in a crisis
- be expected to be at your beck and call.

Unless you're very fortunate, it's unlikely your mentor is going to find you and offer his or her services.

*A coach is normally a paid professional whereas a mentor is usually free. A coach works with an individual or group to identify a specific goal or goals and frames the discussion so as to identify how these goals can be reached. The coach will not necessarily have relevant, specific knowledge and experience.

FINDING A MENTOR:

First identify potential mentor(s); likely to be some
or all of the following:

- positive role model/inspirational
- interesting and interested
- credible with a proven track record
- in a field or circumstances relevant to you
- skilled/experienced/knowledgeable
- a nice person/willing to share
- responsible and responsive
- prepared to build a relationship
- a focused and committed person
- honest and straightforward.

This is a time to make creative use of all the resources available
to you. Think about people you admire, not just those who are
doing the job you want. Look also at those who have similar values
and attributes to your own you could learn from. View everyone
you come into contact with as mentoring potential; who do they
know? Search networking sites; look at company websites and at
business people you know or know of. Tell people you're looking
for a mentor and ask them to recommend people. Follow potential
mentors on Twitter, read and comment on their blogs; don't
overdo it, though, or be over-familiar as you risk putting them off.

Rather than asking outright (especially if you don't know the
person), start slowly and create a relationship. If you plan to
approach a number of potential mentors, by taking things
gradually you will learn who would be most suitable, and you'll
avoid having a number of helpful people who say yes who you
then have to turn down.

You could also make sure you 'run into' your potential
mentor somewhere. You could do something to get noticed
(keep it professional, though). You could even offer to do
something for them.

LOOK FOR THE OPPORTUNITY
AND **TAKE IT:**

As the result of a conversation overheard at an event, I once volunteered to do a piece of pro-bono work for a very successful entrepreneur who, at the time, was chair of a charity and whom I saw as a potential mentor. We spent a bit of time together on the project and he became a mentor for me. Eventually I ended up as a non-executive director on one of his boards. This was all years ago, yet I still see him and his wife a couple of times a year and I know if I needed to, I could pick up the phone and ask for advice anytime. Sometimes he asks me.

That's how relationships can blossom from a standing start.

Anyone could make that happen.

You could play the long game to good effect. Here's a true example:

EXAMPLE:

Joe dropped an email to Breda, a potential mentor in his field: "I've always admired what you've achieved. I'm on track to join the board of my organization within the next year and wondered if you would consider spending half an hour with me to share some of your experiences? I have some specific questions I'd really like to ask you. Or perhaps if you're busy, you could recommend someone?"

Breda's assistant ignored or delegated the email. Joe called to follow up but wasn't successful in speaking with Breda. You might think this would have put him off, though as you probably know it's a pretty common situation. Sometimes the 'barriers' screen out things that the intended recipient would actually be quite interested in.

Joe did regular internet searches on Breda and after a while picked up that she would be speaking at a conference. He attended the conference and made a point of asking Breda if she received his email. Things went from there and Joe secured his mentor.

Sometimes a bit of tenacity and ingenuity may be required.

Or if you're not the sort of person to take the subtle approach, just get on with it and approach your potential mentor and ask them outright.

If people are unable to help, then move on, never take it personally; these are busy people. It's like kissing those frogs – you might have to try a few before you find the right one.

Once you find someone who agrees to be your mentor – and this is **very** important – **you** need to drive and manage the process and make it easy for them to help you.

GETTING THE BEST OUT OF BEING A MENTEE:
Assuming there is every indication you've found the right person, be prepared to put effort into building a business relationship with your mentor. Be open and ready to trust the person you have chosen (and remember that works both ways). There should be an equality of approach; this is not a parent-child relationship, even if your mentor is older and more experienced than you are. You should be respectful and be treated with respect.

It makes sense to set a few ground rules, to clarify the terms of the relationship and the role the mentor will take. You'll also need to agree the housekeeping issues such as how often you'll meet and where – you should at least offer to travel to them (since they are helping you) or meet somewhere in between. After initially meeting, you might talk by phone, Skype, Facetime or other means. Always book the next session at the end of the current one to keep momentum. Some of my mentees just send me emails, which is fast and easy for me and they get what they need without a long meeting. You'll want to concur that discussions are confidential unless you both agree otherwise. Never assume that they will be; there are plenty of examples of mentors 'being helpful' and in the process divulging information that the mentee would not want out there – so make that clear from the outset.

Since you're driving the process, it makes sense for you to plan your meeting agendas and to turn up with a list of topics you'd like to discuss. Some mentors might like to have this in advance, others not; this is where agreeing the ground rules comes in.

Most mentors appreciate a thank you even if it's an email once the work has finished. This extract from an email sent by one of my mentees is a great example of how mentoring has helped her:

... **I'VE BEEN** looking back a lot on my diary notes from all our sessions and done a lot of analyzing. I got offered the job in the Netherlands but, even though I needed a job, after considering the company in comparison to my values I decided to decline the offer, and I feel that I truly made the right decision doing that.

THEN, ABOUT A week ago, I got offered the job I applied for in Reading, the one that matched my values, really well, and I didn't even hesitate when accepting it... I couldn't have imagined a better opportunity. I cannot even find the words to express how amazed I am by how things have changed and worked out .... Thank you so much for helping me, I really enjoyed our sessions and hope that we will stay in touch.

IF YOU ONLY DO THREE THINGS:

1 Be very clear about what you want to gain from the relationship.
2 Work out what sort of mentor is right for you and be diligent in recruiting them.
3 Set the ground rules and build a productive relationship.

| **15** | BECOMING **A MENTOR**

Why give up your time to mentor someone who needs you? Because, as well as the satisfaction derived from helping another human being to become more successful/happier/more focused, you will learn a lot yourself. Mentoring is also a great way to expand your recruitment network, gain additional skills and can provide a useful and refreshing step away from your day-to-day role. Plus, in a small way, you'll be leaving a legacy and many people find that immensely satisfying.

If you're looking to become a mentor, it makes sense to learn how best to deliver; here's my quick guide to help you:

KNOW THE DO'S AND DON'TS:

While you could 'just start mentoring'; I'd advise you to do a little fact finding beforehand so you know what your role as a mentor is and how best you can support your mentee. First think about attributes – take a look at the previous chapter for a list of stuff you should look to avoid. Next search online – there's loads of free information available or you could find a course. If you'd prefer to be connected to a formal mentoring programme, speak to your local university. If they have a formal scheme they will train their mentors and you could take advantage of this by joining their programme, which will benefit both parties.

FINDING A MENTEE:

If you'd like to be a mentor though haven't been approached, put the word out that you'd be happy to take on a mentee. A good place to start is with your general network. Your peer in another department or company would probably be delighted to have your help as a mentor for one of their team. Mentoring isn't necessarily about an older person mentoring a younger one. It could just as well be quite the reverse and, of course, peer-to-peer mentoring is useful and healthy.

WHAT IT TAKES:

Be careful not to become carried away and behave out of character (I've seen this happen – not good). Be yourself – the mentee wants to work with you for who you are.

Mentoring isn't only about guidance; you'll be committing to helping someone develop and progress. While this should not be taken lightly, it can be achieved without spending a lot of time and effort if you manage it in the right way. As well as one-to-one sessions, a good mentor will look for opportunities to provide experiential learning for the mentee. For example, sitting in on a meeting or strategic planning session, being invited along to a networking event, work shadowing/job swap, recommending books and articles and so forth. So be creative and work with what's there already. This is not about you doing hours of planning for your sessions. Remember the onus should be placed on the mentee.

TEN TOP TIPS FOR MENTORS:

1 Only commit to the responsibility of becoming a mentor if you are serious about it.
2 Build rapport towards a confidential relationship where trust is key.
3 Do what you say you will, never over-promise and always follow up.
4 Believe in your mentee.
5 Ask great questions – and allow people to ask you 'stupid' ones.
6 Listen well.
7 Be patient and kind.
8 Be a role model – always.
9 You mightn't have all the answers so work through the options.
10 Remember your mentee is not you and times change; there's more than one way of doing things.

I find that the mentor often learns as much from the mentee as the reverse. This is very desirable and an equitable arrangement and is why there must be a trusting, equal and respectful relationship.

If, for some reason, the relationship doesn't work, then have an honest conversation about that. It may be that this intervention causes the relationship to flourish; if not, give what help you can to finish off professionally and move on quickly.

IF YOU ONLY DO **THREE THINGS:**

1 Take time to get to know your mentee, creating an open and professional relationship.

2 Set the ground rules so that your mentee prepares well for maximum effect.

3 Agree initially on a duration e.g. six months – you can always expand it later.

| **16** | CONFIDENCE, POISE AND **THE X FACTOR**

As evidenced by the placebo effect, and the power of the mind in particular, belief is immense. For those who aren't familiar with the placebo effect, here's an explanation:

THE PLACEBO EFFECT is where a patient is given treatment that they believe to be of genuine medical benefit. He or she expects it to improve his/her condition and be of genuine medical benefit, though in fact it is devoid of health-giving benefits. Even so, it may cause the patient to believe the treatment will change his/her condition and as a result the patient experiences actual therapeutic benefits whereby their condition improves. This phenomenon is known as the placebo effect.

IT THEREFORE MAKES sense to engage the mind in believing in oneself and portraying outward confidence and poise which, in turn, will help trick the mind into believing this to be reality.

Indian leader, reformer and Nobel Peace Prize winner Gandhi once said "If you think you are lesser or greater than someone else, you'll make it reality. We are all born equal, what makes one man president and the next unemployable is how much he allows his thoughts to drive his life."

WHICH TWIN COMES ACROSS IN THE BEST WAY?
GEMMA – a nervous, fumbling, apologetic woman with hunched shoulders and crumpled jacket

Or

EMMA – an upright, confident person who answers questions assuredly and wears a crisp, pressed suit?

They both have the same DNA, the same environmental and social influences, yet Emma has chosen to play the confidence card. Emma or Gemma? It's up to you.

Typical traits of confident people (tick off the ones you have mastered and then work on the rest – practise in the mirror if necessary):

- say what they think
- speak clearly
- hold their head high
- have upright, firm posture
- answer questions assuredly
- know what they stand for
- admit if they don't know
- learn from mistakes
- inspire confidence in others
- go all out to make things work
- take calculated risks
- don't seek praise
- accept compliments with grace
- sit at the front
- speak up
- are happy to help others
- ask questions, listen and learn
- look presentable, dress well/appropriately
- keep fit and healthy
- make a contribution
- smile a lot
- believe their chosen path is the right one
- walk purposefully
- walk fast
- make eye contact
- are prepared to commit
- think things through, plan and prepare
- celebrate successes

- count their blessings
- have a positive attitude
- imperfect but OK with that
- have definite beliefs and principles
- are prepared to trust
- are focused
- push themselves out of their comfort zone.

One of the best ways to become more confident is to take on challenges that you might find difficult. For example, if you dread giving a public presentation (and many people fear this more than death), find a low-risk opportunity to prepare and deliver one. Find someone to mentor you through the process; prepare and practise properly. And then go for it. Volunteer for tasks and experiences that are out of your comfort zone. It's a brilliant way to prove to yourself that you can succeed.

If you're not quite brave enough yet – mock up situations and do them in front of a mirror or play them out in your head. An important technique is to imagine things going well – and you'll probably find that they do. And if you mess up, then who cares? No one's going to die (unless you're training to be a doctor or an airline pilot, in which case ignore this advice and find a simulation opportunity).

The more you practise, the better you'll get, so start today.

IF YOU ONLY DO **THREE THINGS:**
1 Look the part.
2 Adopt the traits of confident people.
3 Believe you can, and do it.

| 17 | ASSERTIVENESS – TIME TO **MAN UP**

As a person becomes more confident and self-assured, he or she is able to be more assertive.

Assertiveness is the ability to express oneself in a way that is honest, direct and appropriate while respecting the point of view and feelings of others. Assertive people stand up for their rights while respecting the rights of others.

If you want to be happy and successful at work, assertiveness is a key skill to master. There's a questionnaire on my website which tests how assertive you're likely to be. It can then be used as a framework for developing the personal qualities that will contribute to your confidence, emotional intelligence and assertiveness of approach.

People who aren't assertive tend to fall into three camps:

1. PASSIVE

2. AGGRESSIVE,

3. PASSIVE-AGGRESSIVE.

Passive-aggressive people tend to exhibit the following types of behaviours:

- non-communication
- avoiding/ignoring
- evading
- procrastinating
- obstructing
- fear of competition

- ambiguity
- sulking
- making excuses
- victimization
- self-pity/'poor me' scenario
- blaming
- manipulative
- learned helplessness
- destroys trust
- gossiping

It's likely that you will be, or have already been, on the receiving end of passive, aggressive or passive-aggressive behaviour from a parent, teacher, work colleague, or manager. The important thing to remember is that people have rights and you will always achieve a better result by being assertive and encouraging those around you to be aware of their behaviour and become assertive too.

OK, so you can't march into your boss's office and demand she becomes less aggressive or more assertive because that would, in itself, be an aggressive way to try to tackle the situation. It would be much better to have a coffee together and tell your boss how you're feeling; discussing how you could achieve better results together and a more positive working relationship, perhaps by communicating in a different way. Of course if that falls on deaf ears then it's your choice to stay and put up with it or to find a place to work where you'll be treated with more respect. Please don't let the put-downs root you to the spot

– it happens and it doesn't have to. If you find you're repeating the same stuff over and over, this is telling you something

– if people aren't listening or prepared to respond then you will need to act. Find your inner cheerleaders and break out of there… You owe it to yourself. Again, life is not a rehearsal.

This is all about rights.

YOU HAVE THE RIGHT TO:

- Ask for what you want (realizing that the other person has the right to say 'no').
- Express your feelings, opinions and beliefs.
- Make your own decisions and cope with the consequences.
- Say 'yes' and 'no' for yourself.
- Change your mind.
- Say 'I don't understand'.
- Choose whether or not to get involved in the issues of someone else.
- Make mistakes.
- Be alone and independent.
- Privacy and your own space.
- Be successful and acknowledge it.
- Change yourself and become assertive.

TEN TOP TIPS FOR BECOMING MORE ASSERTIVE:

1. Meet the person at their level.
2. Speak at a similar volume to the other person and keep calm (or adjourn).
3. Use "I…"/"I feel…"
4. Be prepared to discuss and compromise - "You want X, I want Y, so…"
5. Remember you have rights/equality.
6. Think about what both want to achieve.
7. Be aware of feelings/relax.
8. Use pre-emptive/explanatory statements: "You may not like what I'm about to say…"
9. Think of your role model – "what would he/she do?" – channel your inner cheerleader.
10. Start small and gain experience.

Make sure you are dealing with facts – never make assumptions. All sorts of dramas befall people because of something they think they know rather than what they actually do know. This is particularly true of people who like to give and receive a lot of feedback – they can tend to extend what they think until they believe it to be fact.

MAGNIFICENT MAN-UP MANTRAS AND CHEESY THOUGH CONVENIENT CLICHÉS:

- *How is this helping?* This is a good one if you feel overly emotional, are worrying about something you can't do anything about or are feeling stressed.

- *What's the worst thing that can happen?* Assertive people know what they stand for, have a sense of what's right and make decisions. Writing down pros and cons is a great place to start and if you're still feeling a little uncomfortable ask yourself this important question.

- *Speak to the one person:* If there's an issue to be dealt with, be sure to go to the person who can resolve it. Expending energy talking to others and gathering endless opinions is counterproductive, can be seen as gossiping and, having gained six people's differing points of view, you'll be no closer to a resolution. Go to the source; deal with it.

- *Life is not a rehearsal:* make everything you do count, spending hours or even years procrastinating, letting things irritate you and feeling unfulfilled is a waste of your precious time on this Earth so make some choices so you can make the most of it.

- *You can't make an omelette without breaking eggs:* it's OK to make mistakes; that's how people learn and progress is made. Instead of beating yourself up, ask yourself what you've learned and how you can do it better next time and then move on. Wasting time worrying is not healthy or smart. Most errors seem far worse to you than to everyone else so learn to celebrate your mistakes instead of letting them bring you down.

- *Feedback is the breakfast of champions:* this is cheesy but valid here, so listen up: feedback is not personal. The vast majority of the time it is provided to enable you to grow and improve, so please learn to welcome it as such. If people take time to give it, be gracious about receiving it. This can be particularly pertinent for Generations Y and Z who have often been told how fantastic they are throughout their upbringing and education; so if you're one of them please take note and learn to take it on the chin.

IF YOU ONLY DO **THREE THINGS:**

1 Resolve to become assertive and do what it takes to get there.
2 Take feedback positively, never personally, and learn as you go.
3 Be brave and venture out of your comfort zone.

| **18** | STANDING OUT FROM THE CROWD

Whether you're in a role already and want to progress or at least be recognized for your contribution, or if you're job seeking, there are things you can do to stand out and therefore create a competitive advantage for yourself. Many of the chapters in this book will help you get ahead though this chapter is about simple things anyone could do straight away to up their game.

Employers are looking for people who will somehow make their organization a better place; financially, environmentally, culturally. So you need to portray a personal image and persona that will give them confidence that you're 'the one'.

First it's important you understand the culture and values of the place where you work or would like to work. Study these well, dissect their website, ask people who work there or know about them – what sort of people do well there? How do they look/behave/think? Diversity is a valuable thing so you're not looking to clone yourself – this is more about displaying the attributes within your own character that will resonate with the organization and the people within it.

A **TRUE STORY:**

Catherine, a very bright student, harboured an unshakeable ambition to join the world of City banking. She had all the right ingredients academically and was focused, organized and driven. However, where she comes from there's a pretty particular dress code and since she didn't know anyone who worked in finance, she didn't realize that the way she looked was likely to hold her back.

You might scream in horror that 'it doesn't matter what you look like on the outside', and that is true. However, certain environments have particular values systems and if you choose to enter those professions or environments, then it's likely you'll have to 'fit in'.

Catherine managed to land herself a preliminary interview with one of the big banks. She went out and bought a new suit (a shiny, bright blue mini skirt and tight jacket), she donned just one, modest, pair of false lashes and carefully applied her best make-up. She was feeling confident in the belief that she looked good. And, in one way, she did. However, her inappropriate clothing and overly made-up look was offputting to the traditional bank interviewer and she didn't make it past the first stage.

Again, this may feel morally wrong, and one day things will change, but the world is the way it is and if you want to succeed in it, sometimes you have to choose whether to 'play the game'.

Enter London City employment charity, The Brokerage, who worked with Catherine to sharpen up her image. That was all it took; all the other ingredients were there. She's now happily ensconced on the derivatives overlay desk of a boutique hedge fund in London.

The moral of this tale is that sometimes you have to look and act the part to get what you want even if it might, temporarily and in a minor way, mean changing the way you are. If that's all it takes, isn't it worth it?

Standing out from the crowd is not just about first impressions and the way you look. Though it is worth noting that when former US football player, OJ Simpson, was on trial for murder, he hired a number of image consultants to ensure he portrayed the best possible impression to the jury – first impressions count.

The key way to stand out is through attitude and behaviour. It's generally accepted that attitudes form only one element of behaviour. In other words, how someone actually behaves will depend not only on their attitude towards something but also upon the immediate consequences of a certain behaviour e.g. how others will evaluate the actions and also habits formed through watching others/learned behaviours in various situations. In addition, there might be specific factors, depending on a particular situation, that will determine behaviour. It's the interviewer or selection panel's job to uncover the attitudes behind someone's behaviours because it's likely that attitudes will prevail and eventually the over-riding behaviours will fall away.

This is why people ask situational questions at interviews such as "Tell me about a time when you took a risk" and then follow up with "Why did you do that and would you do the same next time?" Or they might explore your attitude towards something: "How would you feel about telling a lie to get the result you want?" The best way to come through these situations is:

A) To have a positive, ethical and emotionally mature attitude

B) To say what you actually think and believe (To quote Shakespeare: "To thine own self be true")

C) To stay calm and ask a question if it helps you to clarify the point they are getting at.

TEN TOP TIPS FOR STANDING OUT THROUGH THE RIGHT ATTITUDE AND BEHAVIOUR:

1. *Look the part:* find out for each particular situation. Remember that even if people are dressed casually at work, they'll expect you to turn up as though you've made a real effort with clean pressed clothes and tidy general appearance – unless you're auditioning to be in a grunge band and even then you'll be expected to look the part.

2. *Be professional:* see how things are done, be friendly but not over-familiar, be prepared to learn and take feedback. Stay away from personal calls and social networking sites

until you know how things work around there.
Be interested and interesting.

3. *Be enthusiastic:* willing people progress faster – fact. SPA: Stay Positive Always. Smile.

4. *Look for opportunities to show what you can do:* and do it. This might mean coming out of your comfort zone, staying late, using your initiative – whatever it takes, be prepared to give it a go and this will also show that you are willing to go the extra mile. (You don't have to though you want to do well, right?)

5. *Become a good colleague:* dependable, efficient, effective, organized, punctual, a good listener. Help your colleagues out – make their lives easier – a sure way to get ahead. Imagine yourself in others' shoes; learn to see things from their point of view.

6. *Keep it real:* make sure it's clear what you're there to do and what a good job looks like. Don't expect the most glamorous and exciting jobs straight away – put effort in and the work will become more varied, interesting and carry more responsibility as you become more trusted. Remember, though, that most roles contain some routine tasks – that's life. Use these to develop your skills and then challenge yourself to do them faster and better.

7. *Become a relationship builder:* 'collect' people, get to know them, establish trust, be interested in them and remember things about them (even if you have to keep written records – they'll never know). Keep it businesslike and never pushy.

8. *Think things through:* ask for more info if you need it, never assume (useful cliché: ASSUME makes an ASS out of U and ME). Always engage brain before mouth. Become a diplomat.

9. *Respect personal space:* Find out how people like to be consulted; for example, some people might prefer an email to being interrupted. Remember that people will give you time (it's in their interest to help you to get things right)

though this will probably have to be on their terms
– learn the boundaries and ground rules.

10. *Under-promise and over- deliver:* people will be more
impressed if you deliver the report that's due on Friday by
Thursday morning than if you deliver the report that's due
on Friday the following Monday. And if for some reason
you can't deliver on time, give people ample notice.

BONUS TIP: BE A NICE PERSON TO BE AROUND

People stand out through the results they achieve. So be sure
that what you're doing can be measured or evaluated in some
way. OK, so you don't want to annoy people by singing your
own praises at every opportunity, but if you can make sure you
deliver and exceed to targets and goals you are set, that's a great
way to stand out.

Try putting yourself in your line manager's shoes. Who would
you notice: the one who is always positive, asks good questions,
wants to learn and delivers on time to a good standard, or the
one you constantly have to chase, cajole, correct and otherwise
micro-manage? People don't have time to manage others. They
expect to be able to provide the remit, resources and guidelines
and for the required results to be delivered. This is a far more
enjoyable way to work for all concerned so resolve to make it so.

IF YOU ONLY DO **THREE THINGS:**
1 Look the part (having identified what that means).
2. Stay positive, enthusiastic and energetic.
3 Under-promise and over-deliver.

| **19** | FOLLOW-**UP**

This is a general chapter about the importance of making the most of every opportunity while also making an impression – a great way to do this is to follow up.

Suppose you attend a meeting where lots of discussions take place and actions are agreed. Make sure you always, always note down what you need to do, then go straight back and plan it into your schedule. And most of all deliver on time. I cannot tell you how many people go to meetings (virtual or actual), put energy into the debate, agree stuff and then it drops out of their thought process and nothing gets done. Or worse still, there's a frantic scrabble just before the next meeting to catch up with all the action points. Not good. If you know you should follow up, do it – even if no one else bothers, this is about you, not them.

TAKING NOTES IN meetings: never let the note-taking detract from the listening. By writing down every word meticulously, you won't be able to follow the conversation, see the overview and form clear conclusions – you need your brain for thinking, not scribing. So develop a technique of jotting down key words or other aide-memoires. Or learn to mind map – there's a 'how to' guide on my website). If you really need to, you can write up the detail later, though in my view, that's a time waster too; so learn to summarize – it's a vital skill.

Suppose you attend a development or mentoring session. Remember, your mentor is giving up his or her valuable time to help you. So make it easy for them. Go ready prepared with a list of topics you want to discuss – they are not there to 'manage' you or the process.

As well as thinking about what you want to get out of a meeting beforehand, it's important to make the most of the opportunity by making sure you take some action as a result. Think about what you've learned, how it could be put to good use, do it and note it down. Put what you've learned into practice and see the results. Progress is a key motivator and it's unlikely people will constantly tell you how well you're doing. Learn to measure your own progress and development and be happy in the knowledge you're growing (whatever stage of your career you're in). If appropriate, tell your line manager or team about your results (though don't turn into one of these irritating people who crow about their own achievements constantly as this won't do you any favours – it's all about balance and moderation).

If you attend an interview or a meeting with someone new, follow up. Send an email to say you enjoyed the meeting and reiterate the main points (as appropriate). Note down and follow up actions as a result. The number of people who bother to do this is in the minority, so make an effort. Avoid phrases like 'thank you for your time' since this is a tad subservient and pretty old-fashioned. Better to say something along the lines of "I really enjoyed our meeting" or "It was good to have an opportunity to meet you" – far more equal and shows you mean business.

And if you do attend an interview and don't get the job, be sure to ask for feedback. Truth hurts sometimes, though the emotionally intelligent job seeker will know it's better to have the feedback and work on the weak points than to labour on, making the same mistakes. At Purple Cubed we offer feedback to every unsuccessful candidate – far less than 10% actually take us up on it, which is crazy if you think about it – since they'd be gaining free consultancy/advice from people experts. And if you do gather feedback, take it gracefully. We've had the odd aggressive response which doesn't get anyone anywhere and only serves to show that the employer had a lucky escape.

So if you can follow up, do it. It will make an impression, giving people a sense that you know what you're doing, are professional and dependable and that you will add value to whatever you do – a sure way to become more successful, and ultimately happier at work.

IF YOU ONLY DO **THREE THINGS:**
1. Look for the opportunities to follow up and do it.
2. Take feedback gracefully and learn from it.
3. Plan and organize your follow-ups so they always happen.

20 | TESTS, ASSESSMENTS AND **OTHER TRICKY STUFF**

It's likely that at some time in your career you'll be up against some sort of selection and/or assessment procedure. This might be part of the selection process for a new role, be included in a development programme or team build or because you work for a person or company that rates this sort of stuff.

Stay calm. You are who you are and that's to be celebrated, so rule one is: never try to be something you're not. There's no point landing a role because you cheated the test and then reverting to type once you're there. It won't do anyone any favours; least of all you.

Since the familiar is more comfortable than the unknown, it makes sense to gain some experience of various types of test. You'd be surprised how many people have never done one until they start job hunting. This is particularly true of more senior types who've been in a role for a long time and then suddenly find themselves on the job market. If you can get in some practice in a situation where the results aren't career critical, then do it. That way you won't be thrown when the real thing comes along. There are plenty of free ones on the internet.

Some of the tests you might encounter are:
- Aptitude: these are work-related and test a person's skills or knowledge around specific tasks. The responses are objective; there will be right or wrong answers. Generally the differentiation between those who answer correctly becomes the speed at which they complete. These tests are often constructed so that only a small percentage of the population would be able to answer everything correctly within the time allowed. Therefore it's important not to panic and rush through making careless mistakes.

If possible, whizz through first answering everything you know and then go back and spend the remaining time working out the rest of the answers in the time you have available.

O Verbal reasoning: these are very common because many roles expect you to understand, interpret and use written information. Verbal reasoning tests present a number of written facts or a piece of text whereby you'll be expected to understand, analyze, draw conclusions and otherwise interpret the data.

O Numerical: these check an individual's ability to understand, interpret, analyze and use figures and other numerical data in order to draw conclusions, make logical decisions and solve problems. Leaders might be given a set of management accounts to interpret, for example.

O Abstract reasoning: these use exercises based on shapes and other diagrammatic information to test conceptual awareness and lateral thinking – the ability to identify relationships between sets of images, spot trends, and exceptions and to be able to use this data.

Companies should not use personality tests purely as a 'you're in or out' tool because there are many factors that could affect the results. They should be using them responsibly, as an aid to the selection process, whereby they are validated at interview.

STANDARD INTERVIEW QUESTIONS

Here are a few to get you thinking:

1 WHAT COULD YOU BRING TO THIS ROLE/ OUR COMPANY?
This is not the time to be bashful or self-deprecating. Think hard about this question before you attend any interview because even if they don't ask you outright, you need to be getting the information across. You have to sell yourself because if you don't, someone else will. If you're struggling to think of an answer ask a close relative, friend or other trusted advisor.

2 WHY SHOULD I EMPLOY YOU ABOVE THE OTHER CANDIDATES?

a. This is similar to (1) and again you need to be ready with a list of your key strengths – preferably in the context of the role and company you're applying to. Be prepared to back them up with examples.

3 TELL ME ABOUT YOUR WEAKNESSES/ DEVELOPMENT NEEDS:

Be honest, stick to one or two and always turn them into a positive e.g. "Sometimes I can be a bit impatient but it just means I want to get things done and maybe I work faster than some other people".

4 TELL ME ABOUT A TIME WHEN YOU TOOK A RISK.

This can be tricky because some people will want someone who will, others don't. Be honest and illustrate how well your risk paid off.

5 TELL ME ABOUT YOUR WORST FAILURE.

If you say you don't have one, the interviewer will assume you're not being truthful. So give an example and show how you learned from it.

WEIRD INTERVIEW QUESTIONS

It's likely that at some point during your working life you'll encounter weird interview questions. A lot of people get really freaked out about the prospect of being faced with these questions and it causes them to lose confidence, thus affecting the rest of their interview. You know the sort of thing:

1 Entertain me for five minutes…

2 If the Japanese are the smallest race how would you prove it?

3 What do you think of garden gnomes?

4 If you were an animal, what would you be and why?

5 How many piano tuners are there in the UK?

The great thing about these questions is that there are no right answers. So as long as you can respond confidently, with some

degree of logic and determination to find an answer
and perhaps show your humorous side (if the situation allows),
then you can triumph! So please don't waste time tracking
down every obscure question and working out a response
because that would be a ridiculous waste of your time. These
questions are designed to find out if you can think and apply
reasoning, so do just that. Remember they don't need the
definitive response – they want a method for getting there
or a creative reply backed up by some sort of rationale.

Taking the examples above, here are some ways you
could tackle them – better to think up your own responses
since this is about discovering the inner you, but to
get you started:

1. ENTERTAIN ME FOR FIVE MINUTES…

This doesn't mean you need to leap onto the interviewer's
desk and belt out Whitney Houston's 'The Greatest
Love of All' (that one's for Miranda Hart fans). Think
about why the interviewer might make this request.
Sure he or she might be an arrogant twit and you might
decide you don't want to work for someone so egotistical.
Or depending on the position you are applying for, this
could give you an opportunity to demonstrate how you
would handle the situation if put on the spot and left alone
with a group of clients, for example. In which case you'd
have to keep them entertained so they stay interested
in your company. So tell whoever poses this challenge
something interesting about yourself, maybe thank them
for an opportunity to talk and take them through the
reasons you're perfect for the role, or talk about something
you've witnessed, somewhere you travelled to, learned.
The important point is to show yourself in a positive
light, show you are interesting and creative and make
them feel they would trust you with their clients,
colleagues and others.

2. IF THE JAPANESE ARE THE SMALLEST RACE HOW WOULD YOU PROVE IT?

You could take a logical approach and explain how you would prove this statistically – either by researching average heights of the various nations on the internet or you could come up with something more creative like 'Call Diesel, or Levis and ask them what distribution of jeans they sell around the world. Their jeans are sold just about everywhere, so except for the possibility that leg length isn't an exact indicator of overall height they should be able to tell you how tall people are in any given country based on the jeans they sell there'. Or find out from kitchen manufacturers what height their standard worktops are built to and compare these geographically. It doesn't matter – the point is that you stayed calm, had a go and didn't talk complete drivel.

3. WHAT DO YOU THINK OF GARDEN GNOMES?

This one is just about having some sort of opinion that is sensible, rational and not too extreme (unless the situation requires it). So you could say things like:

- They make good profits for gnome manufacturers – margins are good since they can keep producing the same traditional styles and models; there have excellent distribution channels via the many garden centres throughout the country.
- They motivated Elton John to make an animated movie so you could say they're inspirational.
- You'll have to think about what value they offer - maybe they scare away birds, or their bright colours attract bees and butterflies, and presumably they give pleasure to their owners, some of whom might be lonely and perhaps feel as though they're part of the family.
- They're certainly diligent and reliable workers – they're out there in all weathers, toiling at their manual labour, lifting heavy wheelbarrows and fishing for huge goldfish in their ponds.

O They are an affront to style and taste and should be banned.

4. IF YOU WERE AN ANIMAL, WHAT WOULD YOU BE AND WHY?

Again, it really doesn't matter what you choose though perhaps steer clear of extremes like killer shark or mouse unless for very specific occupations that might desire the accompanying traits. The important thing is to articulate the positive traits of your chosen animal so as to show yourself in as positive and attractive light as possible. For instance:

"**Lion** – *a strong, courageous and powerful leader, inspiring the respect of others, also inhabits a pride so can lead a team.*"

"**Dolphin** – *intelligent, friendly, good communicator, team player, cares for the welfare of others, work hard/play hard mentality.*"

These could be viewed as rather predictable responses though, so maybe go for something more interesting. Below are the traits of the animals of the Chinese zodiac to start you off:

O **Rat:** quick-witted, smart, charming and persuasive
O **Ox:** patient, kind, stubborn and conservative
O **Tiger:** authoritative, emotional, courageous and intense
O **Rabbit:** popular, compassionate and sincere
O **Dragon:** energetic, fearless, warm-hearted and charismatic
O **Snake:** charming, gregarious, introverted, generous and smart
O **Horse:** energetic, independent, impatient and enjoys travelling
O **Sheep:** mild-mannered, shy, kind and peace-loving
O **Monkey:** fun, energetic and active

- **Rooster:** independent, practical, hard-working and observant
- **Dog:** patient, diligent, generous, faithful and kind
- **Pig:** loving, tolerant, honest and appreciative of luxury

5 HOW MANY PIANO TUNERS ARE THERE IN THE UK?

You could demonstrate your logical train of thought – for example:

Well, the population of the UK is about 60 million. So let's say 1% own a piano so that's 600,000 pianos. Let's also estimate that a piano tuner tunes about two pianos a working day so that's about 500 pianos a year. So on that basis I'd estimate there are 1200 piano tuners in the UK.

This might, of course be complete rubbish though you will have shown you can think things through and problem solve. If you're not very good at estimation and/or mental arithmetic or holding a logical train of thought, don't embark on this approach. And avoid saying you don't know at all costs. Simply tell the interviewer how you'd go about finding out, for example "I'd find the UK professional body for piano tuners and call them up".

Don't get hung up about these weird questions, this is just preparing you for whatever those tricky interviewers throw at you. Chances are you'll never come across them. If you do, sit up, stay calm and enjoy the challenge.

ASSESSMENT CENTRES

These last from half a day to two or more days and combine a variety of activities tests and challenges (some of which are listed above) to test your performance in a pressurized situation. In addition to your knowledge, skills and attributes, the employer will be observing your interaction with others, teamwork, assertiveness, leadership potential and your general attitude and approach. Some of these are so well constructed that they are fun, informative and help parties decided who is the best fit (if you've applied to Urbanest, for example, you'll know what I mean) .

Above all, be yourself – you have no idea what the selection panel is looking for so listen, think, act and, above all be a good person.

IF YOU ONLY DO **THREE THINGS:**

1. Stay calm, think and learn to enjoy the challenge.
2. Be yourself – they are looking for cultural and role fit.
3. Practise your approach and possible responses – in the mirror if necessary.

| **21** | **ACCEPTING** A ROLE

So you got the job and/or promotion – congratulations! There are a few things to note before you email or otherwise confirm your acceptance.

- Are you feeling delighted, happy, excited, proud?
- Does this new opportunity 'feel' right?
- Do you have all the details to make an informed decision?
- Do you know what you'll be doing, your goals and objectives, what achievement 'looks like'?
- Have you checked out the company and the people you'll be working with?
- Do you like them, or at least feel you'll work well within that environment?
- Do you understand the terms and conditions, hours, remuneration?
- If you're not feeling positive and enthusiastic now – imagine how you'll feel in six months' time. So unless you're in a situation where 'any job will have to do' just to keep your head above water, think before you commit.
- Make sure you get their offer in writing before a) telling anyone b) resigning.

You should, by this stage, have clarified everything you need to. However, if not, it's OK to go back and ask any questions you have – just phrase it in a way that is upbeat and positive.

"I'm really looking forward to getting started, can I just check a few details with you so I have everything straight…?"

It's better to know now, even if it's not good news, than find out once you're there. Some employers aren't particularly transparent and might not reveal all – in which case you need to consider why you'd want to work for an organization like that anyway…

Write your acceptance positively and with some energy – you want the employer to be feeling really good about his or her decision to choose you as well as totally motivated to put the effort into making things work for you. Give them something to look forward to.

Then re-read Chapter 8 about handing in your resignation and do it properly and honourably.

If your role is one within the same organization, make sure that communication between your current line manager and your new one happens. You might think that's not your job, but it's better for everyone if you take the initiative and pre-empt any issues that might delay or otherwise affect your transfer.

A DILEMMA: Accepting one role from company A while you await a decision from your preferred choice, company B: This is tricky because by sticking it out for the ideal role, you might end up with neither. You could call company B and explain the situation to see if they'll at least give you an indication of whether you're still in the running.

If possible, stick it out for a role you can be happy and successful in. Of course the pressures of everyday living might dictate otherwise, but think hard before you take a job that isn't what you really want. Just because generations of people before you did this (as they will repeatedly tell you), it doesn't necessarily have to be that way now.

And if you do accept A and then are also offered B, you could run the risk of damaging your reputation by then letting company A down. Trust and integrity are important considerations, but at the end of the day, your

happiness is important too, so weigh up the options and
potential risks to help you make the right decision.
It's your call.

IF YOU ONLY DO **THREE THINGS:**

1 Ask the right questions during the selection process so you
are very clear about the role when the offer is made, as well as
the values of the company.

2 Send an upbeat and inspiring acceptance.

3 Be aware of your true feelings; stay wise, professional
and grounded.

| **22** | PREPARING **TO START**

It makes sense to get yourself into the best possible state of mind and state of readiness before you start a new role. It will set you up to make a good start and to 'be the best you can be' at this particular time.

If circumstances allow, take a break between jobs; even if it's only a few days. This will provide an opportunity to clear your head, let go of any 'baggage' from the old job and think about the new one. It might sound cheesy but visualizing things going well has a lot going for it. Back to good old Henry Ford: "If you think you can do a thing or think you can't do a thing, you're right".

Before you start, check out the new company/department online – find out as much as you can about:

- culture
- people
- products and services
- clients and associations
- anything else you can find

If necessary, take the opportunity to brush up on your skills and do some reading…

If you're joining a service organization, check out their offering yourself, and if feasible check out their competitors. Being in the know will help you on your way to being successful. Ask your networks what they know and who they know – they might have a good contact for you. Keep it low key – no one wants a high-maintenance new 'friend' or someone who turns up on day one as a bit of a know-it-all – store the information for use at the appropriate time in an appropriate way.

You could offer to go into the work place for an hour or so to meet people before you start. My company offers new starters the option to do this and it certainly breaks the ice; making things easier on day one – especially if it's possible to meet people beforehand in a social context. They might not want you to do this, but there's no harm in suggesting it via email, explaining why you suggested it.

If you need to, organize reliable childcare and/or make sure you and your partner have worked out who's doing what so you're not left panicking. This will help you to separate out your work time from your home life, unless you find a company who will provide childcare facilities or allow children at work and they are in the minority.

Eat healthily and get enough sleep. New job; new start on the exercise front? Well, it's a thought…

Make sure you know when, where and who to report to on day one.

Check out transport options and if possible test out your journey at the time you'll be travelling to work. Arrive early – 9am start means arrive at 8.50 so as to get organized and ready for the day. Remember, you're trying to make a good impression. And if you're going to be late – call them and say so: put the numbers in your phone so you have them to hand.

Make sure you take the following with you on day one:
- Notebook (hard-backed and professional-looking) and pen (smart and definitely unchewed) or other means of recording key points and looking as though you're serious and want to learn/do well
- Your bank details
- Work permit/copy of passport if required
- National insurance/social security number

● If the company is switched on and has sent out your terms and conditions and/or other info, take that too – preferably in a tidy file or folder i.e. not scrunched up in the bottom of your bag (it happens!)

REMEMBER – FIRST impressions count...

Make sure you're equipped with appropriate work wear; you can always 'trade down' by removing a tie/jacket or rolling up your sleeves – it's very difficult to trade up, though. So, if in doubt go for the smart look. Decide what you're going to wear the night before, make sure it's clean and pressed and lay it out ready to step into in the morning. Clean your shoes. This all helps to keep things moving calmly along, rather than having a mini-crisis because a button is missing from your favourite shirt.

Less really *is* more – avoid strong aftershave or perfume, comedy socks or ties, heavy make-up including false eyelashes, blingy nails and keep accessories and jewellery simple and classic.

Pack your bag ready to go. Make it easy on yourself: that way you can put your energy into getting there and thinking about what the day has in store for you.

Stay off the garlic, curry, alcohol, and beans the night before – anything that will make your tummy rumble or taint your breath. And if you're a smoker, stock up on mints – some workplaces are really anti-smoking, so be careful not to go in there wearing 'Eau de Ashtray'.

GO TO BED EARLY!

Have a good breakfast – preferably including protein and slow-release carbs to give you energy. Breakfast is not just for wimps – many studies prove that those who eat a good breakfast are:

LESS:	MORE:
O tired	**O** energetic with more stamina
O irritable	**O** positive
O restless	**O** able to solve problems

ABOUT NERVES

Nerves or excitement? It's the same physical reaction – you'll need to choose to allow your nervous energy to work for you, not against you.

REMEMBER, THEY PICKED YOU – GO OUT AND SHOW THEM THEY MADE THE RIGHT CHOICE.

On the way to work, read the newspaper so you're informed. Reading is an excellent way to broaden the mind and the thinking process so use the journey time to improve your knowledge – unless you're driving, of course; in which case listen to the news on the radio.

By now you might be feeling like a first grade boy-scout – very virtuous. Remember, you owe it to yourself to be the best 'you' you can be and to make the best effort to impress on day one.

IF YOU ONLY DO **THREE THINGS:**

1 Do your homework – get informed, stay informed.
2 Be as prepared as possible – make it easy on yourself.
3 Feel good about yourself and your new challenge; use your nervous energy to work for you.

TWO-THIRDS THROUGH...
WORDS

CONGRATULATIONS
you're now TWO-THIRDS through this book.

Here's a 'chapter light' to keep you going...

As the Bee Gees or maybe even Boyzone famously said,
"It's only words".

There are a few words you should ban from your vocabulary
right now – go for it, you might like it:

TRY: there is no try; it's either you will or you won't. Try is a
get out for I'm not going to but I'd rather not say so. Successful
people do not 'try'. So ban try, now, today, please.

NO PROBLEM: problem is a negative word. By mentioning
problem you're introducing the notion that whatever it is
you're talking about could potentially be a problem. People
often subconsciously screen out the deflective so if I say to you
DON'T think of a purple cube – what do you immediately
think of? Instead of no problem, use a positive statement such
as 'absolutely' or 'of course'

~~DON'T BE NEGATIVE~~ BE POSITIVE!

BUT: This is a pesky creature that has a habit of deleting all the
good stuff that came before it. So If I say "I liked your report
but I'd like you to make some revisions..." it becomes a negative

sentence. Replace 'but' with 'and' as in "I liked your report and now I'd like you to add in some revisions". Also if you ban 'but' it will stop you using it to start a counter argument and you'll have to think of something more intelligent to lead with.

TO BE HONEST: an unnecessary filler and implies that at times you are not honest. This is especially bad for sales people. "I'm not gonna lie" is even worse – stop it now!

IN MY OPINION: another unnecessary filler. Of course it's your opinion since you are the one who is saying it.

DON'T KNOW: Far better to say "I'll find out for you". or "Let me think about that and come back to you".

CAN'T: You can do most things if you have the time/ resources/skills – like 'try', can't is a negative word and a self-fulfilling prophecy.

BUSY: is a good word until you put "I'm too" in front of it. Sounds unhelpful and as if you can't control your workload; lose it and learn to make time.

SURVIVING, THRIVING, **HIGH-FIVING:**

| **23** | YOUR FIRST DAY – AGREEING **THE GROUND RULES**

In the same way that first impressions are so significant when you meet someone, the first day of a new role is an opportunity to set the tone for what follows. If you've taken the advice presented in Chapter 22, you'll already be well equipped, well presented, on time and in the right place.

We always advise employers to sit down with new people and go through the following:

● The job description – more crucially, what does this 'look like'/how will you know if you're doing it as they want it to be?

● What outcomes/results are expected and how will this be measured?

● Values/culture – what's important?

● The non-negotiables/rules – 'How we do things around here and stuff we don't'.

● How best to work together.

Since some employers don't have much of a clue about this stuff (though hopefully you'll be working for someone who does), you'll need to go on a mission to find out for yourself. This does not mean going in there on day one with a list and interrogating your new boss. Unless you have a working relationship with them already or at least good rapport, you'll have to do it gradually and/or ask the other people you work with.

If you're not sure what to do, ask someone; there's nothing worse than shuffling hesitantly or hanging around without purpose. If they're not ready to explain your work, then do something helpful like offering to make the tea. You want to come across as willing rather than creepy, so don't overdo it!

Good employers will design an induction programme for you (and the really good ones will send this to you before you start so you know what to expect). This will make sure all the important things are covered, that you meet the people you need to and are given the tools you'll need to do a great job.

If you don't have this and feel you have been 'thrown in at the deep end' then accept it; man up and make the most of it – find someone friendly and ask questions.

When your work is explained, take notes – however bright you are, there's no way your excited brain will remember everything. Taking notes will show you are committed and mean business. The way you're asked to do things may be different to what you've been used to. Learn to jot down key points so you can maintain eye contact, listen properly and ask for clarification when required.

- Avoid the temptation to compare the new way with what you've been used to. Never assume you can do things the way you did before unless you've discussed this specifically.
- You're in a new environment so adapt.
- Go with the flow – do what's asked; once you've proved yourself and earned people's trust, you can set about presenting your ideas and/or adapting the work.
- Be modest – never brag about what you did before.

Attitude first:
- You don't have to prove yourself on day one – better to become a person who's adaptable and good to be around; you can wow them with your skills, abilities and knowledge later.

- Criticizing your previous employer won't do you any favours either so keep the past in the past unless there's a really good reason to bring it up.
- Be willing to learn and willing to act – these people employed you to get results.
- Have energy and enthusiasm; put in 100% effort – people will notice even if they don't say so.
- Be positive – moaning and groaning to fit in with others will do you no favours.
- Avoid compensating for nerves by making silly jokes – be emotionally mature.
- Join in, begin to form good working relationships with colleagues (this will also help you uncover the unwritten rules).

Find out the rules around use of personal mobiles, the internet, and social media including use of email, Twitter and Facebook. Although part of everyday life for many, these are banned in some workplaces so check out what's acceptable before you go online.

Remember what got you the job when you meet new people. Be confident; introduce yourself– don't wait for them to do it. Think:

- Smile
- Eye contact
- Firm handshake

It is NEVER OK to greet new colleagues with any sort of physical contact other than a handshake. Work on making sure your handshake is firm, dry, non-crushing and never wet-fish like!

Someone I know – a tough and high-powered head of human resources for a large organization – was recently totally unimpressed (and somewhat revolted) when, upon meeting her for the first time, a new member of the leadership team leaned forward into her personal space, gave her a bone-crushing handshake with both hands and then kissed her. This seemingly small incident, which made her feel violated and caused everyone witnessing it to cringe, has really affected the perceptions people have of this person and he's going to have to really work hard to come back from it. If in doubt, keep things totally professional, businesslike, and equal while respecting the hierarchy.

Many organizations, especially smaller businesses, may expect you to be flexible about the hours you work. This works both ways. Find out before you take the job what's expected so there are no unpleasant surprises. Above all, avoid being a clock-watcher – no one likes a person who objects to doing a little extra occasionally. Before you leave on day one, ask "Is there anything else I can help with?"

At the end of the day, always check your schedule for the next day and write your to-do list. This way you will be ready to hit the work as soon as you come in.

ONE DAY RITA was attending the theatre. The play started at 7pm and her working day officially finished at 6pm. The day before, Rita had gone to the fuss of arranging with her colleagues to come in half an hour later so she could finish at 6.30pm and therefore have less time hanging around. That's perfectly within her rights, but Rita missed an opportunity to work half an hour extra and get ahead, and she ran the risk of being thought of as petty and a time waster by her colleagues. Was it really worth it?

Adapt to the culture around you – if people are flexible, be flexible. If people have lunch together, join in. If people like to put their heads down and concentrate on the work, do likewise. If they have a chat about last night in the morning, take part. Or make your excuses – that way people will know you respect their culture though you have valid reasons for doing something different. "I'd love to catch up, but I need to finish my report for John". If you're joining a large organization from a small one or vice versa, please manage your own expectations – it will be very different; watch and listen so you can adapt quickly.

BEWARE THE DISENGAGED

There may well be people who are suffering a disconnect from the company/its culture/their colleagues or leaders. These pesky creatures often hone in on new people to try to get them on side. The best way to deal with them is to acknowledge their opinions/gossip or even bitchiness non-specifically – "Oh, that's interesting" – and move on. Never be drawn or offer an opinion. Above all avoid gossip; keep neutral until you've formed your own opinions as to what's what. The best policy is to be nice to everyone and treat them politely, kindly and with respect.

If you reach the end of day one and haven't enjoyed it, or even worse are feeling you've made a terrible mistake, prepare to give things a chance. If there's something fundamentally wrong, unethical, or illegal then of course speak up. Otherwise, bide your time and see how things go for three weeks. At the beginning write down what you don't like and, crucially, what you would like to see instead. Then see if you can influence this. At the end of three weeks, review your list and act accordingly. Never, ever just walk out – news travels and you don't want a reputation as a quitter. Always voice your concerns and give the employer an opportunity to put things right and/or explain to you why things are the way they are.

TRUE STORY: DO YOUR HOMEWORK

Leo joined the graduate programme of a high street recruitment consultancy. He hadn't really 'done his homework', having become somewhat enamored with the idea of becoming a 'consultant' and of not only advising employers though also helping people to find great jobs. What he didn't realize was that recruitment in this company was essentially a selling role with lots of research thrown in – no consulting at all. At the end of week one he felt he'd made a terrible mistake. He felt the panic rising and thought it would be best for everyone if he were to quit. Then he calmed down and, since there was a formal review set up at the start of week two, he decided to be honest and explain how he felt. Leo did this carefully and positively, taking responsibility for not having researched the role content thoroughly enough. His supervisor persuaded him to do two more weeks and then they would review and decide the future. At the end of Leo's third week, he'd struck up a good working relationship with the supervisor and had responded well and quickly to the challenges she set him. His supervisor saw that he had good potential and was prepared to work hard, giving the role his best shot. He realized that he had a lot to learn and this would be a good place to do it. They agreed a way forward that would develop Leo without being primarily sales-focused. This was over 10 years ago and now Leo is a top billing recruitment consultant with a salary to match and he loves it.

IF YOU ONLY DO **THREE THINGS:**
1 Find out what's expected of you and deliver.
2 Keep your mind open and opinions closed.
3 Do what you can to fit in and gain allies.

| 24 | BUILDING **REPUTATION**

The point of building a positive reputation at work is that
you will be happier and more successful (unless you are
working for the forces of evil or maybe in just a not very nice
place). You owe it to your personal brand to take action to
enhance your reputation.

IT'S A QUESTION of Jon or Edward – who has the best reputation?

JON	EDWARD:
hardworking	lazy
helpful	selfish
trusted and trusting	difficult and shifty
honourable	a gossip
reliable	unreliable
conscientious	uncaring
positive	pessimistic
an initiator	slow to act

OK SO IT'S a total no-brainer, but many people routinely display
Edward's behaviours at work and then expect to get on.

Think about how you're perceived at work – self-awareness
is an important attribute to nurture and will serve you
well throughout your career. Without being needy or looking
like an attention seeker, ask people how they feel you could
improve at work. Be aware, however, they won't always give
it to you straight. Some companies have formal feedback
mechanisms and tools such as 360 degree reviews; if so, be
brave and use them.

If you're unable to gain outside opinion then you'll have to rely on your own self-critical approach. Think about how you'd like to be perceived, make a list and then score yourself 1-5 where 1 = 'not at all like me' and 5 = 'very like me'. You'll probably need to think of examples to help yourself be realistic with the scoring. This will give you an idea of the areas where you have work to do.

List your unique selling points (USPs) i.e. the things about you that are unique – or at least unusual. (These are answers to the interview question "Why should I employ you over all the other applicants?") Then build on these.

Enhancing your reputation at work is a lifelong journey, so start today by doing one thing to build your personal brand. Play 'brownie-point bingo', using the diagram on page 120.

Few managers like to be presented with 'problems' if the person presenting them hasn't a) attempted to resolve them first b) thought through and presented the options or c) if they do it in a stressed/weepy/panicky/aggressive way. So if something needs to be dealt with, stay calm, gather all the relevant information, think about the options and implications, decide your preferred course of action presenting your findings rationally and unemotionally.

YOUR ONLINE REPUTATION

Put your name into a search engine as see what comes up. If it's those dodgy Facebook photos again, the 'secret' blog where you rant about your manager/company/colleagues, or your Twitter feed dedicated to a love of teddy bears, then do all you can to clean up your online image.

Join LinkedIn and/or other online business networks and build up a positive profile. Keep this up to date – many employers look for their next hire this way or at least check them out.

Challenge yourself to take on something out of your comfort zone	Present a solution or well-thought-out options rather than a problem	Copy someone who is respected and capable (though avoid stalking anyone!)	Think things through	Solve someone's work issue for them
Do something without being asked – even if it's only tidying the store room	If you see little things that need doing, do them rather than think 'it's not my job'	Sit at the front at company conferences	Pick up the empty drink can outside reception	Do something before you're asked (and then when they ask tell them you did it already)
Over-deliver – even if you have a challenging workload (it's worth it to impress)	Be low-maintenance and emotionally mature	Leave personal stuff at home	Be positive and receptive	Gather knowledge – become a trusted advisor
Be kind and nice to people	Earn respect – it's not a given	Remember: it's business, not personal	Use your tact and diplomacy to smooth over a situation	Be brave and stand up for what you believe
Think ahead and be proactive	Become the 'go to' person for advice	Present as though you should be running the company (even if that's a long way off)	Stay positive and calm in a crisis	Take a new person under your wing and make them look good

FEEDBACK

Some people will expect more feedback than others. Good organizations will review progress and provide constructive criticism to provide development and keep things on track. The best way to deal with this is not to expect to be told every day that you're doing a great job – busy people just don't have time for that. Make sure you have review meetings planned in so you can check how things are going. No one's going to praise you for 'just doing your job' – they might, though, if you do something over and above it. So assume all's well unless you hear otherwise and, if you're not sure, check. If you receive what you perceive as negative feedback, more often than not it's because the giver wants you to be the best you can be. It's not personal – so be grown up; take it on board graciously, resolving to improve. Above all, avoid being 'needy' – no one loves a whiner.

And if you blot your copybook and damage your reputation:

- act fast
- do what you can to contain the damage
- if you've messed up, put it right – even if you have to put in extra effort to do this
- admit your mistake and say how you're going to move forward
- take the valuable lessons and get over it
- put your energy into resolution, not absolution.

TRUE STORY: A DOWNWARD SPIRAL

Toya had always been a little insecure. She'd struggled a bit at school and had had a couple of bad relationship break-ups. When she started work in the finance department of a large law firm, she did her best and, as a result, received plenty of positive feedback. This really did make her feel like a new, more confident person. As time passed, however, Toya's good performance became the norm and people stopped thinking about giving praise and feedback. Toya's boss, Clifford, was a self-regulator who had never felt in need of feedback himself because he always knew internally if he was doing a good job (or not). He therefore didn't think that he should give Toya feedback as long as all was well; he assumed she was fine and might feel patronized or undermined if he kept commenting. Toya became increasingly more nervous and insecure. She began complaining to colleagues about Clifford, routinely telling them about her achievements, asking busy people for their assessment of how she was doing. This began to irritate others, wasted time and eventually began to demotivate the whole department.

Clifford found it necessary to have a straight talk with Toya. She was mortified to find out that people viewed her as needy and immature and began to understand what had happened. She realized that becoming self-sufficient and confident in one's own abilities is all part of the maturation process. She understood that to keep progressing, she would have to find an 'inner-compass' through self-assessment and regulation, only asking for feedback if doing something that was new or she was unsure of. It took time to rebuild her relationships with Clifford and her colleagues. Eventually Toya moved to a new company but she took with her valuable lessons she had learned, which enabled her to start anew in a more emotionally mature and self-assured way.

IF YOU ONLY DO **THREE THINGS:**

1 Work on your self-awareness and emotional maturity – be open to change.

2 Do one thing every day to build a positive reputation.

3 Admit mistakes early enough to minimize them and do all you can to put things right.

This chapter is included because increasing your stamina and attitude towards being active can significantly impact your success and happiness at work – in a very positive way. I honestly believe that if you want something enough and put enough energy into it, you will succeed – it's all about determination, focus and stamina.

| 25 | STAMINA

I'm going to tell you a true, personal story, because this is one of the factors to which I attribute my ability to get things done and juggle the many 'hats' I wear. I found out early on that in the same way a marathon runner trains his or her body, you can do the same with stamina to give you energy for life.

When I was at college, I took a summer bar job on the island of Jersey in a busy entertainment complex. The hours were long, but the money was OK and it seemed like a good place to spend the summer, have fun and build up some funds for the next term. A typical day went like this:

07.00AM – 08.00AM	BREAKFAST
08.00AM – 10.30AM	CLEAN AND STOCK UP BAR
10.30AM – 11.00AM	LUNCH
11.00AM – 15.00PM	BAR SERVICE
15.00PM – 18.00PM	BREAK
18.00PM – 02.00AM	BAR SERVICE

So a 16-hour work day, one day off a week and an early start or miss breakfast. The first day I sloped off to bed in the afternoon to catch up on some zzzs; the thought of functioning on five hours' sleep seemed impossible. (And I obviously wouldn't recommend it for a sustained amount of time because proper rest and recharging are important.)

On the second day, as I again headed for the dorm, the more experienced hands asked where I was going; told me not to be such a wimp because I'd be missing out on all the fun at the beach, on the island, on the water. So I changed my mindset, put the hours in, had a brilliant time in those afternoon breaks and on my days off, instead of sleeping through them, I learned to water ski, fish for lobster, I ate in fab restaurants, met interesting people, visited other islands… And guess what, I really didn't feel tired – I learned that if you're motivated and having a good time, tiredness doesn't raise its ugly head. It certainly built up my stamina and I've been thankful ever since, which is why I'm telling you my own story. By putting in the effort, it's possible to achieve more, feel healthier and more fulfilled, keep on achieving and fuel your determination and drive.

And I'm not the only one who thinks so. In a recent *Time Out* interview, acting extraordinaire Sir Ian McKellen (Magneto in *X-Men* and Gandalf in *The Lord of the Rings* and *Hobbit* films amongst many other fabulous roles) was quoted as saying:

"If you run and take exercise you have more energy; the same with work: the more you do, the more alive you feel and the more work you want to do. Slip away and sit in the chair and you're probably going to go to sleep."

You don't have to 'go mad in Jersey' to build up your stamina, though. Think about building up gradually, pushing yourself to put in the extra effort in the gym, in sport, at work, at play, take a part-time job, do some volunteering, start studying, help someone out…

It's an interpretation of 'use it or lose it'. So be active, do new stuff, train your body to be energetic when it needs to be. You don't have to knock yourself out à la McKellen – work-life balance is important too. However if you choose to get to the top in certain professions, by virtue of the fact that not everyone gets there, you may have to 'walk the extra mile' (or several hundred). In time you'll begin to enjoy the challenge of building yourself up; this will help you to get through tough times and the sense of achievement is a real boost in itself. It becomes a lifelong thing – if you want to fit in lots of good stuff, then you have to choose to make the time.

GO ON, I CHALLENGE YOU...

IF YOU ONLY DO **THREE THINGS:**

1 Change your mindset from 'I'm tired' to 'I can do anything'.
2 Take on some extra activities to build your stamina and staying power.
3 Enjoy the challenge and remember you are training your body to help you do well.

3

> **BONUS TIP:** Celebrate how far you have come.

| 26 | COMMUNICATION

This is a massive general subject, which underlines its level of importance in the workplace. Most conflict and issues are caused by a lack of communication or miscommunication. There are no rules to say you will receive excellent communication at work so it's up to you to take responsibility and find stuff out if you need to.

If you've ever played Chinese whispers at a party, you'll know how messages can easily become corrupted. (If you don't know what that is, there are some funny examples on YouTube.) Most successful people are good communicators – they provide clarity; simple messaging so that people can understand them and are clear about what they need to do with the information. Start now to hone your comms skills. Here are some hints and tips:

1. Think through the result you want and how you can get there (think in bullet points for clarity) – this way you can be clear about the points you make.
2. Start with the recipient in mind – think about how best to put the point across, use examples and facts to back up what you're saying. Tell stories to illustrate your message.
3. Aim your communication at the right person i.e. the one(s) who can do something with the information – examine who the key recipients are.
4. Use the best, i.e. most appropriate method, for each situation.
5. Decide what style to use; informal or formal, overview or detail.
6. If it's a potentially tricky one, think it through or role play with a friend.
7. Get your timing right (and never procrastinate).

Plus, in one-to-one or multi-way exchanges:

8. Clarify any actions and/or conclusions so the point of your communication is clear.
9. Make sure you follow up.
10. Set an adult-to-adult tone and have trust and belief until proven otherwise.
11. Listen and ask questions, summarizing as you go, check understanding, take notes.
12. End on a positive note.

THE MEETINGS MYTH:

All meetings are necessary, productive, stimulating, equal, grown-up. Many meetings are quite the opposite – so if you're attending meetings that you dread, do something about it. There are people who love having meetings for meetings' sake ("It's so nice to get together"); there are people who believe decisions must be made by total consensus. This rarely works in practice so if you're included, enhance your reputation by doing some thinking beforehand which could cut down the discussion and give a valuable starting point. If appropriate, make sure there's a clear agenda to avoid trawling through what's happened before, and use the meeting for forward thinking and decision making. Prepare a meeting plan for those attending with allotted amounts of time for the points to be covered; this will help prevent discussions going off-track.

THE 4MAT SYSTEM

The 4MAT System comes from a study of learning styles by US learning expert Bernice McCarthy. She noticed that people learn and take in information in different ways. Some people want to know Why, e.g. why are we doing this? What's in it for me? Others like the facts question, e.g. what is it we're going to do? Some are more interested in the detail and how things will happen, e.g. How does this happen? How does this work? And some want to know what if, e.g. What would happen if I did this?

4mat is therefore a brilliant structure for almost any communication or presentation because it captures the attention of all types and gives everyone what they want to know. The structure is therefore (in this order):

1. Why
2. What
3. How
4. What if

Starting with 'why' provides meaning, excitement, relevance and engages the recipient – in many communications, the why doesn't come until the end, by which time you've lost interest; instead people start with the what or even the how. Stating why is particularly relevant when it comes to Generation 'why' Y. 'What' provides an overview of the subject and is great for low detail people (possibly your boss) who isn't all that interested in the how. The 'how' provides more detail.

Ending with 'what if' reminds the recipient that this is a good idea and they will get something useful out of it. There are some examples on janesunley.com.

READ THE MOOD in the room – are people listening, nodding their heads (or otherwise)? Adapt your approach to keep them interested and on your side. **YOU CAN'T DO** this if you're reading from lots of notes so learn how to speak from the heart, using notes as a prompt.

PRESENTING TO A GROUP

Audience: think about the group and what will get them excited and interested – talk their language, think of stories and examples they'll relate to. Each person takes in information differently, whether verbal, visual or through experience. Do your best to ensure there is something for everyone.

Topical and relevant: be clear and make sure you can fit all key points into the time available. Avoid cramming in everything you know – stick to three key ideas.

Method: if you must use slides, use images to illustrate your point and, if appropriate and at all possible, bring some humour.

Never read out text from a slide (and I mean NEVER, unless you're referring to figures, tables etc). Keep it simple, high impact and energetic. For each slide make 1-3 key points and learn these – this avoids having full notes which are easy to lose track of and it looks less polished. It also avoids repetition.

Interact with the audience: talk to them as if you're having a conversation – expect and encourage them to answer back.

Check they're still 'with you', check understanding, and seek feedback - "Does that make sense"? "How does that sound to you?"

And remember, practice makes perfect. If you know your stuff and can communicate it clearly then it is more likely the audience will be engaged, will interact and will take action afterwards.

EMAIL ETIQUETTE

1. Before you write an email, consider whether a phone call or face-to-face would give you a better and/or quicker result (and provide an opportunity for a bit of bonding).
2. Email is for quick replies so reply quickly (our rule at the Purple Palace is by the end of the day). If something requires more attention and can't be dealt with that day, reply to say when you'll be dealing with it, put it in your calendar/diary and do it.
3. Be disciplined to deal with email every day. Make sure that by the end of the day you have no more emails in your inbox than are visible without scrolling down (we call

this 'Inbox Zero +10'). Be organized and don't become a slave to email at the detriment of progressing other work, though – there is an off button.

4. Use the subject bar properly so it is very clear what the email is about e.g. instead of 'Budget' write 'January 2010 budget (info)'. Only use 'Urgent ' or a red flag if it really is – in which case phone or face-to-face is probably better.

5. This will save loads of time: Consider putting your message into the subject bar only so the recipient doesn't even have to open the email. In this case you need seven small though powerful words to use in brackets after the message:

- Saw a great account manager and appointed today (End)
- Bar and restaurant budget figures need re-forecasting due to Michelin star (Action)
- Sales figures 40% up this quarter (Info)
- Attending the HR meeting? (Confirm)
- We screwed up the proposal we're presenting tomorrow – when can you meet? (Urgent)
- Group budget (Summary)
- Pub on Thursday after company meeting (Social)

6. Keep text short and focused, use bullet points and always make it clear what you require as a response. Read through before you send for a sense check. Emails to clients and head office should be checked twice.

7. Use email for positive messages only; problems should be dealt with by other means. Keep the tone even and friendly yet professional. **NEVER USE CAPITALS – THEY SHOUT!!**

8. Never write anything you wouldn't want to see on the front page of the local paper or that you wouldn't say to someone's face. If there's something sensitive to deal with, avoid doing it by email.

9. Think before you 'cc' (copy people in) – only send messages to those who really need to know to

avoid clogging up people's inboxes. Ditto with the 'reply to all' function.

10. Only attach items that are essential. If people use mainly smartphones, post short attachments into the email under the main message.

BONUS TIP: Delete all spam, chain letters, jokes and unknown attachments – never forward them on.

SOCIAL MEDIA

I'm not going to go into detail here because you know the score. However, please remember that anything broadcast via a social networking site like Twitter, LinkedIn, Facebook and YouTube can potentially be seen by the whole world, so take care and use them to your advantage. You could set up a group for your employees/colleagues which could significantly enhance the communication process. You have to maintain it though and make sure it's fed with rich content or better to leave well alone. Be careful about using Twitter if you've been on a 'good night out' – what seems sensible at the time could cause major embarrassment the following morning.

IF YOU ONLY DO **THREE THINGS:**

1 Be accountable – good communication is everyone's responsibility.

2 Think in bullet points so messages are clear; remember the 4mat system.

3 Check through any written communication and put yourself 'in the recipients shoes'.

27 | GUIDANCE, SUPPORT AND **FEEDBACK**

In an ideal world you'll be working for an organization that:

- specifies from the start what's required, how you can contribute and how this will be evidenced
- offers clear guidance and support
- is prepared to let people do things their own way (freedom within a framework)
- gives regular, constructive feedback – both positive and remedial
- has a regular review/appraisal system (it might even be online so you can use it throughout the year)
- has an open and trusting culture where people feel secure about giving and receiving feedback
- believes in its people and their abilities.

However, you might well find that this is not the case. And if you're job hunting, do what you can to measure the above before you accept a role as this will save you a whole lot of hassle in the future.

Finding the right balance between gaining feedback, guidance and support and being perceived as a 'high-maintenance, self-obsessive' is not always easy, but is definitely worth the effort.

TRUE STORY: COMPROMISE
FOR A WIN-WIN

Lia's first job after graduating was in a busy advertising agency. She was looking forward to learning lots and becoming a valuable part of the team. However, the culture was very much one of hectic, high pressure and last-minute deadlines. She found work was more or less thrown at her and she was just expected to get on with it, finding out herself what was needed in order to do a good job. She only ever found out if she'd done something wrong because all of her good work seemed to pass by unnoticed. She felt miserable and almost gave up. However, this was her dream job - she'd beaten hundreds of other candidates to get it and, despite feeling like the office dogsbody, she was learning a lot fast.

Lia decide to stick it out for at least an 18-month period with a view to using her experience to move on. In the meantime, she decided on several coping strategies as described in this chapter.

REMEMBER, SOMETIMES IT'S WORTH THE COMPROMISE TO GET WHAT YOU WANT FROM A WORKPLACE... FEW WORKING ENVIRONMENTS ARE PERFECT.

Eventually Lia gained the respect of her colleagues and superiors. She began to value the trust they put in her to get things done without needing help. Just as she was coming up to her self-imposed deadline to move on, she was offered a well-deserved promotion and ended up staying with the agency for another three years. During this time she was able to change the culture a little; helping new people have a better experience than she did...

First think about feedback on a need-to-know basis as opposed to a needy basis. Some people are fortunate to have an 'inner barometer' whereby they know if they're doing OK (or not) – some need feedback on everything and spend lots of time asking people questions.

I believe the right place is about 25% from the inner barometer point (left below):

I KNOW
how I'm doing

I NEED FEEDBACK
on everything

In today's workplace, if you go too far to the left of the above diagram you're in danger of being so self-assured that you don't notice when things need to be improved. Anything right of centre and you're likely to be edging towards 'just too needy'.

If possible, establish early on (i.e. before you join or start a new role) how things are done with regard to:

- **Guidance:** is there a job description? Are there guidelines and goals? Is it clear how things are done around here?
- **Support:** route to ask for help? Trusted to get on with it? Mentoring/buddying?
- **Feedback:** open culture? One-to-ones? Regular reviews?

If none of this is in place, yet you have good reasons for wanting to join, you'll have to be resourceful about fulfilling these needs for yourself – without alienating you or anyone else. It becomes your choice to live with things as they are (or not) and find coping strategies such as:

1. Asking how specific things are done as the need arises (it helps if you can befriend someone who's happy to help or share it out so you're not bugging one person the whole time): "How best can I contribute?"
2. Establish ground rules by checking the way you're thinking of doing things is OK "I've been thinking through project X, when would be a good time to run through my questions with you?"
3. Realize that in some cultures feedback is minimal and only when negative (this is a prime example of an occasion where you'll have to 'man up' or move on).
4. Be honest and open: "What could I do better next time?"; "What would you like to see?"
5. Use self-improvement as an excuse: "I've decided I'm going to improve XYZ and I'd really appreciate your feedback".
6. Establish trust by becoming reliable, sincere and unemotional.

7. Ask someone how they would have done it; listen and act.

8. Find out how success is measured – "What does a good job look like?"

9. Find a colleague and strike up a mutual deal "I'll support you and give you feedback if you do the same for me".

10. Be resilient – awarding yourself praise and feedback.

Above all, you do **not** have to:

a) be perfect

b) know everything

c) do everything right all the time.

Be open to guidance and feedback because you want to be the best you – if you receive criticism, resist the urge to interrupt or be defensive, listen, hear them out, thank them, then do something positive with it.

And if you do need to challenge, then do it only when it's important – no one likes an over- defensive complainer.

A really good way to ask for help and guidance without appearing needy or high-maintenance is to make suggestions to resolve the situation and put the onus back on the person asking for the work. Instead of using "I need: more time/more resource/someone to help…" phrase it like this:

"I know that project X is business critical so I've spoken with Joe who can finish off project Y for us."

"I can do project X in three days and project Y in two days yet they were assigned with a Friday deadline date. Which deadline would you like to extend?"

You'll need to work on your emotional intelligence and assertiveness skills for this approach so read Chapter 14.

IF YOU ONLY DO **THREE THINGS:**

1 Remember where you work is a choice; if you choose to be there, work the system to acquire what you need.

2 View feedback as an opportunity to learn and grow.

3 Work on becoming self-assured – you do not have to be perfect.

28 | BULLYING, BITCHING AND **BELLIGERENT BOSSES**

Bullying at work is an unfortunate fact of life. It can be defined as any behaviour that causes anxiety, intimidation, belittling, forced control or feelings of inadequacy. This is sometimes linked to culture; whether something is acceptable or not can lie with the recipient. If offence is taken by a particular event or comment, then it's unacceptable. If in any doubt whatsoever, don't go there. And of course, it is never acceptable to single someone out because of their age, sexuality, nationality, sex, sexual orientation, disability, or personal characteristics; or to be straight, just because you don't like them.

I really hope you never come across bullying at work. If you do, here's a plan for dealing with it:

> **ABOVE ALL: AVOID** feeling guilty. Being the victim of bullying is not your fault.

1. Think about the instances – be very objective; is this bullying and what examples can you give? Write them down and look at them very dispassionately. Some bullies don't know they're doing it; others take perverse pleasure in their bad habit. Be careful not to confuse constructive feedback, shyness ("she blanked me") or general inadequacy with bullying.

2. Remember this is not because of any shortcoming of your own; it is the inadequacy/fear/envy/insecurity/immaturity of the bully that is the root cause.

3. Take action – nipping things in the bud before they get out of hand will save you much stress and anxiety in the long run. You owe it to yourself. Avoid gossiping, though you

should discreetly check with trusted colleagues how they feel about the situation (you might not be the only target).

4. If you do feel you're being bullied, have an 'off-the-record' chat with the bully – preferably in a relaxed environment e.g. over coffee. It may be that the bully isn't aware of the effect. Many bullies put their insults and jibes down to 'banter'. This is not acceptable. Explain the results of this interaction in an unemotional, factual way describing how you feel rather than what he/she did. It may be that pointing out the issues and agreeing a way forward will solve the situation. This takes a degree of assertion and courage, but it can be so worth it if you consider the alternative…

5. If you really don't feel you can deal with a face-to-face discussion, as a last resort before making it official, you could write a polite note, though be careful to keep it light and factual – you don't want the tables to be turned on you.

6. Be careful not to join in or try to play the bully at his or her own game.

7. If, having met with the bully and agreed a way forward, things don't change, give fair warning that you feel you have no alternative than to take it further.

8. Go to someone who can help (this could be your line manager, department head or human resources team) – explain the situation in terms of lost productivity, how business/company/team profitability, reputation, team dynamics and so forth are affected. Make sure you have accurate, valid examples from your earlier notes to illustrate your points.

9. Know when things have gone too far – you may decide to transfer to another department or even leave – remember, though, your employer does have a duty of care to deal with negative situations like this. You may wish to take legal advice before you resign.

10. If you're feeling stressed or ill, get help. Remember,

no job is worth your health. Be realistic and reasonable,
though – no one likes a person who blames everything from
a cold to an ingrowing toenail on their job.

TRUE STORY: BANTER OR BULLYING?

Nick worked in a busy IT development business. The founders of the company
had rather old-fashioned ideas about what's acceptable in the workplace. There
was much swearing and rudeness, much of it levelled at Nick as the 'new boy'.
When he raised his objections, it was put down to 'banter' and Nick was told to
get on with it and grow up.

After one particularly nasty incident when his boss was unacceptably rude, belittling Nick in front of a valued client, he decided to leave. He probably could
have taken up a case at an employment tribunal and would almost certainly
have won. (At the time of writing, the UK compensatory awards are between
£12,900 and £72,300.) Nick chose not to and so the company avoided a fine
and a loss of reputation. However, they also lost an excellent employee and a
chance to improve their working practices. I wonder how many people Nick
has told about his experiences…

BITCHING:
This is a form of bullying. Although often less trivial in content,
it is not necessarily trivial in its end result. Some people like
gossiping and 'having a good bitch' – it becomes a habit that is
hard to break. Once endemic within an organization's culture,
it's tough to eliminate. Some people are bored and do it just to
fill time; others have more sinister reasons. The most important
thing is not to get drawn in.

With the subject of bitching, the best defence is resilience –
ignore the gossip. However, if this starts to have a detrimental
effect on your health, self-esteem, happiness or performance,
then take action as per the previous plan.

A good plan is to discuss the situation with a trusted colleague. They may be able to advise and you might even find they feel as you do. This is often better than going straight to the top – it's difficult to continue any sort of positive working relationship with people you've reported to the management; they might not even realize the effect they're having. This is the start of working together to come up with a strategy to deal with the perpetrators. It might be as simple as sitting down and explaining how you feel and agreeing some ground rules.

Communication is key. If you're not happy with something that's been said, then say so assertively and evenly – avoid any sort of judgemental superiority – say it the way it is and see what happens. And say it to the one person who can make the change, otherwise you too can easily fall into the bitching trap too.

Remember, you have the right to work in a safe and professional environment and you don't have to stay there if you're unhappy and cannot resolve the situation.

USEFUL CLICHÉ:
NEVER work for
a bad boss

BELLIGERENT BOSSES:

Like beauty, what makes a bad boss is in the eye of the beholder. If you're not sure what's acceptable, here are a few of the signs of a bad boss:

- stroppy and over-critical
- takes credit for your work and ideas
- mad about rules and rigid in the 'how to's
- behaves inappropriately
- doesn't deal with issues
- doesn't think things through
- lacks trust – believes in guilt before innocence
- undermines confidence
- negative
- knee jerk reactions/takes comments at face value

- tells secrets
- intrusive
- hyper-critical
- no feedback or
  thankyous
- picky and petty
- poor rapport with others
- plain unfair.

AT THE TIME of writing, an internet search for 'bad manager' resulted in 827 million responses. On the basis that most people are essentially good, whose fault is it that there are so many bad managers?

OK, so no one's perfect and you have to remember that being the leader can be very challenging, pressurized and often lonely. So you might need to be forgiving of a few of your boss's less-than-perfect traits, managing upwards to help you cope. However, if the person you work for is routinely displaying three or more of the above and you're beginning to feel weary and demotivated, then unless you're in a role/company/environment/situation you absolutely love, then you might want to ask yourself why you're still there. Remember, you have a choice. You deserve to be happy and successful.

USEFUL CLICHÉ: 'PEOPLE leave people, not companies'. To most people their line manager IS the company — no matter now amazing the CEO is, this is lost when a bad boss lurks.

Sometimes your boss might not know he or she is upsetting you. The lack of leadership development, mentoring and positive role models over the past decades has taken its toll on general leadership capability. Bad bosses probably learned their behaviour from other bad bosses. So see if you can break the cycle. Be brave and have a frank talk about how better you could work together to get a superior result. You might be surprised by the outcome.

Bad bosses are not to be confused with tough, inspirational people who have high standards and are driven, focused and determined to get a result. These are good bosses because they provide clarity about what needs to be done and drive the organization to the required outcomes.

IF YOU ONLY DO **THREE THINGS:**

1. Stay calm, stay rational and take action if you're unhappy.
2. Write down the situation, where you'd like to be and think about how you could get there.
3. Remember, you have the right to be happy and safe at work so if you can't get things satisfactorily resolved, move on (it's their loss).

29 | REVIEWING YOUR **PROGRESS**

Ideally, your employer will have in place some sort of formal and informal feedback mechanisms. This is especially important in the first three months of your role since this is the vast learning curve which, handled well, will set you up for happy and successful times ahead. In our company we sit down and have formal two-way conversations on weeks 1, 2, 3, 4, 8 and 12, and then our formal online review progress kicks in. Others will do things differently. The important issue is that there is some exchange of feedback and ideas and that goals are set and progress measured.

If you find yourself in a place (maybe in a very creative environment) where the formal approach is shunned, do not despair. This is the trade-off for being in an environment you love. You need to learn to review your own progress (see also Chapter 24).

WHY BOTHER?

Progress reviews are important to:

- make sure you're going in the right direction and doing the right things
- check you're making a contribution and progressing
- ensure action plans are working for the business
- correct minor mistakes and keep on track
- discuss any development needs and decide how they'll be fulfilled
- provide self-reflection
- discuss and agree next steps and explore ideas
- give and receive feedback on a range of issues
- provide insights and form bonds.

By reviewing your own progress you'll not only be sure you're progressing, you'll also have evidence of your worth within the organization. Self-reflection is critical to development; but, whatever you do, don't go into 'analysis paralysis' and start measuring everything and anything. Keep it simple and quick. You'd be better off putting your time and energy into doing than into measuring stuff.

A quick and simple way to measure progress is as follows:

1. Write down what you're there to do (if you don't have a clear, simple job description).
2. Write down other important factors (see suggestions below)
3. Write down how this can be evidenced (in overview; remember the 'analysis paralysis').
4. Review your progress, noting down examples and evidence.
5. Decide what you'd like to do better/what's next.
6. Revise your action plan.

And so on...

Your organization will no doubt have some hard measures in place such as profitability, sales figures, gross profit percentage, spend per customer/per square metre, income per head, items produced, numbers processed, interviews held, employee turnover and so on... Make sure you're aware of these metrics and what the actual results are for you, your department and the company. For many organizations, profitability is the key concern, so make sure you're on the right wavelength when it comes to 'the numbers'.

Some softer factors you might like to review (choose no more than five):

- attitude
- skills
- knowledge
- personal presentation and style
- methods of working
- organizational skills

- ability to 'get things done'
- reliability/punctuality/conduct
- commitment
- whether your way of doing things is compatible with the organization
- creativity/innovation.

And so forth… this is not an exhaustive list. The key is to find the traits you need to have to perform well and measure them. Ask yourself – if I was doing 'X' to the required standard, what would it 'look like'?

Another great thing to do is to do a bit of a 'self review' every day or even every week. Reflect on your day – you could do this before you go home as you're writing your to-do list for the next day (see Chapter 23), on your commute or whenever suits. It's satisfying and motivating to think about what went well, what you've achieved. What are you particularly proud of? What did you enjoy? What do you wish had gone better?

And you're not doing this to 'stack up evidence', though if you build your own, evidenced portfolio of achievement it's sure to come in handy somewhere down the line…

IF YOU ONLY DO **THREE THINGS:**

1 Use any feedback mechanisms that are in place.
2 Make time for objective self-reflection.
3 Remember: the outputs are more important than what you did to get there (especially to your action-centred employer).

| 30 | LEADERSHIP MUST-HAVES (EVEN IF YOU'RE NOT ONE)

How many leaders and managers do you know who are disorganized; who are poor communicators; poor problem solvers; lousy team players?

My next book, *Leaders At All Levels,* is based on the idea that if everyone developed basic life skills including those that leaders need, the working world would actually require fewer leaders and would therefore naturally gravitate more towards self-managing teams. This fits perfectly with Gen Y's reluctance to lead in the traditional sense.

I'm giving you the heads-up now on how to become more successful and gear yourself up for the team dynamics of the future.

There are certain traits that you'll need to work on. Some of these are listed below, though the often overlooked 'school of the how not to' is very useful here in defining what you need to know. Observe leaders and managers in your organization and note the things they do well and where the gaps are. I'd be willing to bet these will be simple skills such as running meetings to time or remembering to do stuff. Note these down and they will form the start of your leadership 'must-haves'. It doesn't matter if you have zero aspirations to lead a team of people in the conventional sense; believe me, they'll be invaluable in the future for self-managing and for working collaboratively with others. And if people did this stuff anyway, they'd be more effective and efficient; there would be less need for managers and certainly no micromanaging – now there's an interesting prospect…

To give you an idea of the sort of traits you could be developing, below is my list of essential leadership traits. There are lots, so best to start now! Of course, this is just my definition

– there may well be others depending on you
and your circumstances.

LEADERSHIP TRAITS AT PURPLE CUBED

WHY: We want our leaders to be the best they can be; inspiring role models for those around them.

WHAT: Top five leadership traits agreed at leaders group last year.
These spell C-CORE:
- Clarity
- Charisma
- Outcome focus
- Role model
- Emotional intelligence

HOW: These have been expanded to further define them and clarify the behaviours required of purple leaders. This will form the basis of Purple Cubed's leaders reviews and will also be the focus of our formal development sessions:

CLARITY
- Clarity: being a clear communicator, especially in emails and meetings.
- Always 'making it simple'.
- Big picture: being able to take an overview, considering, but not bogged down by, the detail; reaching the right, purple, decisions.
- Organized: able to plan, work efficiently and effectively, inspiring the same in others.

CHARISMA
- Being an inspirational leader, giving clear guidance and displaying role model behaviours, allowing freedom within a supportive framework.
- Confidence: leading from the front, being brave and strong, self-assured, with poise – inspiring, comfortable stepping outside personal comfort zone.
- Positive personal attributes: a strong and diverse set of skills and characteristics plus an unwavering purple attitude, exemplifying the purple image and impact.

OUTCOME FOCUS:

- Decisiveness: being sure of what to do in a timely way – not procrastinating, happy to challenge the norms.
- Goal focus: able to set goals and make them happen, focused on achievement.
- Proactivity: able to anticipate the opportunities and pitfalls, always thinking ahead to create the best outcomes.
- Financial awareness: understand the numbers and able to influence them.
- Sense of urgency: things are dealt with quickly and appropriately without fuss.

ROLE MODEL:

- Being purple: living the values and putting purple 'paint' on everything they do.
- Progression: able to learn and grow, evolving with the business and those within it.
- Judgement: doing the right thing, being wise and definite about things, having an opinion.
- Resilience: able to make the best of a situation; remaining strong, focused and upbeat in the face of adversity.
- Commercially savvy: always mindful of the goals and acting in the best interests of the business, encouraging the same in others.

EMOTIONAL INTELLIGENCE:

- Self- awareness: being aware of others' perceptions and own impact.
- Emotionally aware: always able to adapt to the situation, empathetic yet strong, sensitive towards others, able to resolve conflict swiftly and harmoniously.
- Positive: strong and spirited; emotionally consistent; always able to find the upside.
- People skills: interested and interesting, able to create strong relationships, someone people want to spend time with, fun.

WHAT IF: Enabled and self-sufficient people with the tools, skills, support and enthusiasm to grow the business.

IF YOU ONLY DO **THREE THINGS:**

1. Understand that everyone needs basic leadership traits because the world is changing.
2. Start developing in these skills (yourself and in others).
3. Keep a log and evidence your success – celebrate!

31 | GETTING STUFF DONE AND A SENSE OF URGENCY

This is a biggie. In fact, I'd go as far as to say this is one of the most significant chapters in this book. It might sound simple and obvious, but the ability to deliver is far too rare a commodity in today's working world. There's so much 'BS' flying around that sometimes people forget what's important.

If you want to be happy and successful at work, your chance of success will be much greater if you master this simple yet desirable way of living your life. There is a big secret to all of this:

> **YOU CAN GO** on as many time-management courses and listen to as many self-help gurus as you like; getting things done comes down to two little words: SELF-DISCIPLINE.

Yeah, yeah, I know it's boring, but you'll thank me one day because it makes complete sense. Most people know how to go about being efficient and effective; the issue is that most people lack the drive to put in a consistent effort so as to become organized; a dependable person who delivers.

Suppose you've got a few things to do; how do you remember them? You keep them in your head, right? No, no, no! You cannot afford the luxury of keeping stuff in your head; heads are for thinking, not storage. So **lesson one** is to always write stuff down (or note it on your handheld device; though I have to tell you crossing through stuff on a written list when you've done it is somehow more satisfying – even to a Gen Y).

A good method for this is:

O Plan everything you can into your diary – remember you may have to review and adjust your priorities (refer to lesson two below). This also ensures you'll avoid having one of those demotivating, ongoing, overly long to-do lists that never seem to end.

O Every evening before you leave, write your to-do list for the next day – by doing this the work ahead is clear and you can choose to think about it, which is a good way to prepare. Tidy your workspace.

> **USEFUL CLICHÉ: 'TIDY** desk, tidy mind' – people notice and you'll feel better and more businesslike.

O Be realistic about what you can achieve and move tasks to your diary for the future if you're looking at an impossible workload. This is where the self-discipline comes in.

O Cross off your tasks as you complete them.

O Always BANJOE – bang a nasty job off early (this is very motivating and energizing as you get the nasties out of the way first).

O At the end of each week, review the next week and make sure what you have planned in is 'do-able' – remember to leave time for reactive tasks, then write your next to-do list as normal.

O If there's just too much to do and you're sure you're working as effectively as possible, don't suffer in silence. Talk to your line manager about reallocating some of the work or getting more resource (very important point: you have to be businesslike and matter of fact about this, proving the business case, and never whiney).

If you're the sort of person who just reacts to stuff and that seems to work well for you, I'd implore you to adopt a more disciplined approach. I've tried it both ways and I have to tell you that the seemingly boring yet disciplined approach makes for less stress, more control, better reliability, fewer working hours, more leisure time, better results and a more successful career – it's a real no-brainer…

Lesson two is to prioritize using the grid below. Many people waste time on things that are neither urgent nor important because they're trying to please others or they simply enjoy doing them. See what I mean about self-discipline? If it's urgent and needs to be done, do it; getting a sense of urgency about you is very advisable – it separates the 'men from the boys' figuratively speaking. Urgency is not to be confused with panic – urgency is about being fast and resolved yet measured.

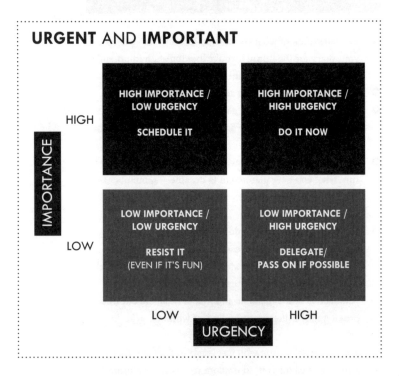

URGENT AND IMPORTANT

IMPORTANCE

HIGH

HIGH IMPORTANCE / LOW URGENCY

SCHEDULE IT

HIGH IMPORTANCE / HIGH URGENCY

DO IT NOW

LOW

LOW IMPORTANCE / LOW URGENCY

RESIST IT
(EVEN IF IT'S FUN)

LOW IMPORTANCE / HIGH URGENCY

DELEGATE/ PASS ON IF POSSIBLE

LOW   **HIGH**

URGENCY

Which brings me onto doing stuff for others. A really good mantra to live your life by is: 'under-promise, over-deliver' – this means if the report's due for Friday, deliver it on Thursday.

Or if someone asks you how long a project will take and you estimate it will be four months and then you deliver it in three, they'll love you forever. This is a super-easy way to impress people and it costs nothing. Let's call that **lesson three**.

Another important lesson (that would be **lesson four**) about doing stuff for others is to learn to say no without using the word no. Once people find out you are an efficient and effective type, they will start asking you to do things for them. If you take on all of their work (especially if you're a nice person who wants to help) you will end up lacking the time to do your own. You will become stressed and this will affect your own productivity and motivation levels. You owe it to yourself and to your employer to say no. So how about:

- **O** I'd love to do that for you though I have work planned in until next Wednesday, can it wait till then?
- **O** I can do X though I'd have to ask you to do Y for me.
- **O** I'd really like to support you though I'm already working late three nights this week to clear my own stuff.
- **O** I want to help though I have a whole load of deadlines of my own, sorry.

You get the picture – this is where the self-discipline comes in and (note the absence here of the word 'but'; see page 110) you have to be ruthless with your time because it's in such short supply.

You can't deliver if you're not clear on the outcomes of course; make very sure you understand what the finished job looks like. So **lesson five** is to make sure you are clear about the deliverables and how they will be evidenced. You have no idea how many people set out to do something with a fuzzy brief and then things go wrong, they feel bad, in fact everyone feels bad, time's wasted, motivation suffers – and it's all so completely avoidable with a little bit of planning and agreement ahead of

USEFUL CLICHÉ: 'PROCRASTINATION is the thief of time'. People spend ages dallying around and worrying about the mammoth task ahead or tormenting themselves about what might go wrong. The important thing is to take things one step at a time and get started as soon as you know what needs to be done. One step flows on from another.

diving in. So if the person giving you an assignment is unclear, ask the right questions so you know exactly what the brief is. A good, succinct format for any brief is to use the 4Mat system (see Chapter 26):

1. The why: the point of this task, the overall outcome.

2. The what: what it is that needs to be done (in overview).

3. The how: this may well be the responsibility of the person who is doing the task though some guidelines are always helpful (especially if the person giving the task has specific expectations).

4. What if: what a good result will look like, what contribution it will have made.

If something happens to upset your schedule, never wait till the last minute in the hope that things will 'just work out' – unless you're prepared to put the extra hours in. So **lesson six** is to communicate and manage expectations. People will be impressed and you will appear in control, which is a good way to be.

And there ends **lesson seven**.

IF YOU ONLY DO THREE THINGS:

1 Be self-disciplined and adopt a system that works for you.

2 Be assertive about not taking on everyone else's stuff.

3 Keep sight of urgent vs. important and be disciplined about it.

32 | ENTHUSIASM AND MOTIVATION

WHY IS ENTHUSIASM SO IMPORTANT?

Well for a start, work is more fun if you and others are feeling enthusiastic and motivated as opposed to bored, fed up and generally lacking stimulation. Enthusiastic people radiate positivity and therefore are more attractive to others – they'll want to be with you, work with you, support you and follow you.

They are also people who get stuff done, overcoming obstacles and challenges (viewing them as stepping stones to success instead of confining them to the hypothetical 'too difficult' box).

They display positive body language and tonality and so communicate in a more compelling way.

They are cheerful and grateful for what they have, yet always on the road to improving, developing, progressing, making a good contribution.

They are happy and successful at work and love their jobs.

Enthusiasm and motivation at work are very much about choice. If you're not feeling it, then it's important to remember that you:

a) should be
b) have a right to be
c) have choices and
d) have a responsibility to yourself and your employer to be.

You know those really annoying people who seem to have it all? Up at 5.30am to go to the gym before work, yet they still somehow have time to always eat a healthy breakfast. They are successful and happy at work yet also fit in a host of other activities and commitments. They have amazing energy and never say they feel tired or short of time.

They are not a weird freak of nature. The big secret is that they are not very different from you. The distinction is that they make choices and take action to nurture incredible energy levels so as to feed their enthusiasm and motivation levels. And they don't allow anyone else to influence this. Pretty much everyone can do it – it's all about choice and keeping energy and positivity up.

If severely disabled Sophie Christiansen, who has cerebral palsy, can win three Paralympic gold medals – on a horse no less – then you don't have much of an excuse really, do you?

USEFUL CLICHÉ: USE it or lose it

START NOW WITH A CONSCIOUS DECISION TO IMPROVE YOUR MENTAL STATE.

The good news is: there are lots of ways to be enthusiastic at work:

1. Get your energy levels up – the more you do, the more energy you have.
2. Eat properly, get enough sleep and don't get wasted every night.
3. Do what you like doing – if you hate your job it is pretty much impossible to be enthusiastic.
4. Arrive early and raring to go (if you did your to-do list the night before you'll be focused too).
5. Take responsibility: choose to be positive, warding off negativity at all times.
6. Have goals and targets for yourself, keep track.
7. Celebrate your achievements.
8. Like your company and your colleagues.

9. Strive to be the best – work out what that 'looks like' to you.
10. Learn, develop, grow, progress.
11. Hang out with positive people, work for a positive person.
12. Be careful who you listen to – screen out the naysayers.
13. Think about things that make you feel enthusiastic
    and recreate them.
14. Be a genuinely good person; always easy to be around;
    patient, tolerant, reasonable.
15. Examine feelings of annoyance, conflict, negativity and put
    your energy into prevention instead of anger.
16. Introduce appropriate high-energy actions at work: high-
    fiving, woo-hoos and lots of laughs – you know the stuff
    (OK, you have to watch out for the 'Cheese Police' so do
    what's appropriate to your culture).
17. If you don't feel so enthused, pretend otherwise because
    perceptions often become reality.
18. Walk tall and purposefully; walk quickly; get more done
19. If issues in other parts of your life are affecting your mindset
    at work, deal with them.
20. Smile and have fun, listen to rousing music, dance and laugh.

You can see that this is a holistic approach to the issue. If it all
seems a little daunting, choose one and perfect it before moving
to the next – you have to keep it up, though. This is like dieting
versus healthy eating – only the one where habits really change
actually works.

CHOICE: THE ONLY people in life you cannot choose are your family
– the rest are there by preference (and don't have to be).
THOUGH YOU CAN'T choose the events around you, you can always
choose your reaction.

MOTIVATION:
This is not something that is 'done' to people; it is a state of
mind over which they have control. It is not the manager's job

to motivate you. He or she can provide inspiration, guidance, support and the right circumstances (oh, and not behave like an idiot); you still have to keep yourself motivated.

When people lack motivation at work there are a number of undesirable behaviours. Below are some of them. This is certainly not a negative book; I'm telling you about this so that if you recognize these in yourself or others, you can do something about it:

- blaming others
- making excuses
- not taking responsibility
- lack of faith
- fear of failure
- low self-esteem
- lack of confidence
- disinterest
- procrastination
- disorganization
- overly problem-focused
- defeatist
- lacking purpose and goals
- out of control
- nervous
- stressed
- under incentivized
- lacking pride
- under-achieving
- gossiping, complainer

You only have one life and you don't deserve to spend it on any of the above so do something about it. A good approach is to write a list like this:

ISSUE	WHAT I WANT	WHAT ACTIONS I COULD TAKE
Not getting on with my boss	To be allowed to use my skills and expertise instead of being micro-managed	Book in a meeting to discuss better ways of working

Sometimes you'll find that the reason you're not happy is that your personal values are not being fulfilled (see Chapter 4); in this case, more drastic action may be necessary. And if this all seems too daunting, then talk to someone about it: a friend, trusted colleague, mentor, family member, your doctor or other professional. Above all – do something.

Ways to be more motivated at work:
1. Check out all the information before you take the job.
2. Prioritize/organize your time.
3. Know your goals.
4. Mark your accomplishments.
5. Find meaning in your work.
6. Set yourself challenges; be the best you can be.
7. Use and develop your skills and expertise.
8. Communicate well and ask the right questions.
9. Make sure you're happy with the rewards and recognition.
10. Look for cultural alignment.

IF YOU ONLY DO **THREE THINGS:**
1 If you aren't enthusiastic or motivated, take action.
2 Remember you have choices, so make positive ones.
3 Fake it till you make it – decide you are going to behave as an enthusiastic and motivated person, even when you may not feel 100%.

33 | LEARNING AND PROGRESSION

Many people feel as though they are not developing if they aren't receiving 'training' in the traditional, classroom sense. This has to stop. Few organizations have the resource to send everyone on endless courses and most employees don't want to learn this way or don't have the time to anymore. Of course, classroom learning has its place, though we always think of it as a last resort rather than the first port of call.

You're going to need to take responsibility for your own learning and development – never assume that it will be handed to you on a plate. And if you can't find out what you want to know, then ask for it, always making the business case – your employer needs to see what the return on investment will be – how this will advance the business and not just your career. Of course some organizations provide development that is not business critical as a motivator, but this is not the norm.

TRUE STORY: GET REAL ABOUT LEARNING

Tim joined a well-known international company in his third job after graduating. He'd been on a fast-track programme in his previous role with formal classroom sessions and online theoretical learning (which had helped him land this one). After a few weeks he complained to his mentor that he just wasn't learning anything. When they explored this statement it transpired that, while Tim hadn't undergone any formal learning and development, he had actually picked up many new skills, polished a few existing ones, gained very valuable experience and acquired a lot of knowledge. The issue was that Tim's employer hadn't put a formal plan in place or formally reviewed Tim's progress.

As a result, Tim designed his own development plan. This consisted mostly of stuff that could be learned and experienced on-the-job plus some self-study. He kept his own learning log and thought about how he'd know if knowledge and skills had been acquired so he could tick them off his list. Tim's manager then agreed to put in a monthly review meeting so they could discuss his progress. This was very welcome, but having now taken responsibility, Tim also knew that if his manager hadn't agreed to do this it would have been OK because he was becoming more self-reliant and able to manage his own progress. This is a very valuable thing.

Here are some of the low-cost/no-cost ways to develop:

ON-THE-JOB	Work it out, ask a colleague, watch others, try stuff out
READ	Magazines and other media, business books, even books like this one
SELF-STUDY	Look for distance learning, Open University courses, attend events and seminars (your employer might help you fund this if you prove the business case)
INTERNET	This is a brilliant resource because you can find anything (remember it doesn't automatically make you an expert though)
JOB SWAP	With a colleague or further afield
VISIT A COMPETITOR	Costs nothing and very enlightening – do it on your own initiative and impress with your findings
PROJECTS	Volunteer, ask for them – remember this must add value to the business too
ROLE MODELS	Watch them, emulate them (but avoid becoming a stalker)
MENTORING	Find a mentor or buddy at work, or look outside for a role model type who will help
E-LEARNING	This might be available at work or maybe you'll have to make a personal commitment – the upside is that's it's usually low investment
MENTORING	See Chapter 14. Also, reverse mentoring is a great way to learn. This is when the mentor learns from the mentee – something I do a lot
CSR (CORPORATE SOCIAL RESPONSIBILITY) ACTIVITIES	Volunteering, be it some community work or becoming trustee of a charity, is a great way to expand your knowledge and gain new contacts

ATTENDING A CONFER-ENCE	Industry or more general events often give access to great speakers for relatively low outlay
AND, OF COURSE	
DEVELOPMENT COURSES	Research role-specific courses and, if necessary, put together a business case as to why you'd like to participate and how the employer will see a return on the investment

LIFE SKILLS:

As a priority, any individual should consider his or her 'life skills'. These are the building blocks of becoming happy and successful at work and will significantly enhance performance and learning. A life skill is one that will enable better performance in life and enable you to work towards your full potential. There is no exhaustive list and key skills will vary depending on circumstances, beliefs, culture and even location, so here are a few of our favourites. If you can master these, your life will be a whole lot more straightforward:

- **Writing skills:** people who can write well are usually logical thinkers. Good writing ability is a tremendous skill to have in all parts of your life – help it along by reading a lot.
- **Listening:** the ability to listen, consider and form conclusions. Linked to this is…
- **Questioning:** asking the right, pertinent questions and at the right time, assimilating and probing the responses.
- **Critical thinking:** being reflective and thinking in a reasonable and rational way so as to make assessments, decide what to do, what choice to make, what to believe.
- **Numeracy**: even a basic grasp of numbers is essential to most roles in the commercial world.
- **Communication:** ability to give information in a clear, succinct and appropriate way (and see listening above).
- **Interpersonal skills:** harmonious and suitable interactions with others.

- **Employability:** see Chapter 13; it's all about being the best you.
- **Problem solving:** an important skill, which involves understanding the issue, exploring options, deciding upon a course of action; which brings me to…
- **Decision making:** being decisive and committed to a course of action (and recognizing and then changing course if it proves not to be the right way).
- **Assertiveness:** see Chapter 17 – being firm yet fair.
- **Negotiation:** the ability to arrive at a 'win-win' through understanding, assertiveness and compromise.
- **Service:** is not just for waiters; the ability to give service to colleagues, your manager and others is just as important as providing those memorable customer experiences.
- **Big picture:** learning to see the overview is a valuable skill (think wood and trees).
- **Self-discipline:** the ability to participate and have fun while knowing when to say no and preventing situations from 'going too far'.
- **Body language:** learning a few basics such as smiling, standing proud, and sitting upright makes such a difference.
- **Emotional intelligence:** being able to control and regulate your emotions is a massive advantage – it doesn't mean being devoid of feeling; it means being appropriate, relevant, calm and reasonable.

And then we come to common sense, which is not at all common. Some people dislike this phrase, but maybe they're the ones who don't have it. Common sense covers a multitude of very useful abilities. It's about being able to simplify a situation; using inherent, sound judgement to do the right thing.

IF YOU ONLY DO **THREE THINGS:**

1 Remember that learning is a lifelong process.

2 Take responsibility for driving your leaning, accepting that the execution is down to you.

3 Look for low-cost/no-cost methods and grab the opportunities.

34 | TEAM DYNAMICS AND **HAVING FUN**

You might be the most qualified and talented individual around, but unless you are in the unusual situation of not having to work in any sort of a team, you will find work, well, hard work, unless you can function well as part of a team. There are two main aspects to teamwork:

1. Being part of the overall team, committed to the same ideals, values and common goals. An example would be the following story which, although often told, still rings true in illustrating a person's sense of purpose and alignment with the common goal:

AN OLD CHESTNUT of a story: During a visit to the NASA space centre in 1962, President Kennedy came across a janitor carrying a broom. He interrupted his tour, went over to the man and said, "Hi, I'm Jack Kennedy. What are you doing?" The janitor responded, "I'm helping put a man on the moon, Mr. President."

---

2. Belonging to a specific team where people are united in order to fulfil a goal or goals.

The two are not mutually exclusive.

In order to be a good team player, in the broader sense, it's good to understand the main common goals and smart organizations will articulate this to their teams. As an example, Google's purpose is:

"To organize the world's information and make it universally accessible and useful."

Some organizations call this a vision or mission statement –
if you want more information on that, you could always read my
first book, *Purple Your People*.

Some organizations have very complex statements that no one
really understands. It's probably not your job to challenge that
right now though, so as long as you can find a sense of purpose
within the context of your organization and what it does, then that
will be fine for now. The important thing is that you know how to
make, and that you are making, a contribution. If this isn't the case
then think about why you're there at all.

Whatever the case, think about yourself in the bigger picture,
just like the janitor at NASA; instead of defining what you're
there for by task.

If you choose to work within a team environment it is inevitable
that you will need to serve the bigger picture. If this isn't your thing,
then consider working for yourself, work your way into a senior
role where you can delegate but not participate, or find a role where
you can be alone and/or work in a more isolated way.

SPECIFIC TEAM DYNAMICS:

The A-Team was a 1980s TV series, more recently revived as
a movie. It features a crack team of four fictional characters.
Here are their profiles:

JOHN 'HANNIBAL' SMITH: a brilliant tactician and master
of disguise. He thrives on adventure and life-threatening
situations; an optimist, enjoying every sticky situation the team
get into. The leader of the team, his catchphrase is
"I love it when a plan comes together".

TEMPLETON 'FACEMAN' PECK: an absurdly good-looking,
suave sweet talker. He serves as the team's con man and
scrounger. He scams, hustles and cons his way into procuring the

information, supplies and equipment needed for the various heroic challenges the team encounter.

BOSCO ALBERT 'BA' BARACUS: an excellent mechanic and general Mr. Fix-it as well as being the one responsible for discipline. He is an all-round tough guy, a huge muscled man who is adept in all forms of defence. He drinks milk, never alcohol and is a regular Mr. Nice Guy, until roused into action. BA has a fear of flying which results in the others rendering him frequently unconscious in order to transport him by air.

H.M. MURDOCK: The best helicopter pilot in the Vietnam War, he is deeply unstable and either mentally ill or pretending to be. He is needed because of his insane levels of bravery and fantastic flying ability. Although interned in a psychiatric hospital, he frequently escapes to join the A-Team's missions. His insanity manifests itself in various ways, which makes him unpredictable. He has an invisible dog called Billy.

The A-Team is an excellent example of a high-functioning team consisting of very distinct, and sometimes dysfunctional, individuals. Although no one team member is perfect, or possesses all the skills and attributes needed, as a whole they bond together to form an unbeatable force. You can see how important it is to define individuals' personal traits, experience and abilities and to work out how best they can work together in harmony. I, for one, would not be allocating the strategic planning to Murdock, nor would I be asking BA to fly the helicopter.

So work out how you can best contribute and work with others to get the job done. In order to be able to do this, you'll need to understand the goal; what needs to be done and what the end result looks like. How you'll know when you've succeeded. If this isn't clear, ask. Sometimes managers don't make the time to think this through. If they don't, then take the initiative, do the thinking and offer it up for their approval.

If at all possible, define the team, who's involved; their strengths; what they bring to the 'mission'. What competencies are required and who possesses them. Then together you can work out how to use everyone's strengths in the best way. If you're new, you might need to appear passive in this – just do it in your head and ensure you use your own strengths to best effect.

Good teams communicate well, allocating individual responsibilities so that they can then come together as a sum of the individual parts. They plan the steps of the journey and monitor progress, celebrating the milestones. Less effective teams all muck in together and hope everything will somehow get done. If you're not clear what your role and responsibilities are, what you need to do, by when, then find out. Good team members listen, share information and are flexible. They give and receive feedback. They are committed and prepared to respect and support their fellow team members.

The A-Team had a lot of laughs during their many missions, so if you're in a position to influence this, make it fun – a happy team is a productive team. People spend about 100,000 hours at work during their lives, so it stands to reason that they should be enjoying those hours. You don't want to turn it into a comedy club though, so balance is key – 'work hard, play hard'. Here are 30 suggestions for enhancing fun at work that I've experienced or seen in action. If you're not in a position to use any of these now, save this list for the future:

1. Have lunch together.
2. Tell stories (helps new people feel part of the success story).
3. Use humour to get the point across.
4. Manage time so there's less stress and more time for fun.
5. Share books and discuss them.
6. Learn a language – maybe a multi-lingual member of the team could teach the basics of their language?
7. Learn to dance together.

8. Take part in sweepstakes for major sporting events such as the World Cup or Olympics.
9. Introduce fun warm-up exercises for team meetings.
10. Get everyone to email round their top three achievements at the end of each week and introduce a fun element as the 'PS'
11. Avoid taking things too seriously.
12. Offer a reward and recognition programme that acknowledges 'above and beyond' service or work.
13. Introduce a fun budget for treats or activities – which is managed by the team, not the manager.
14. Join in with the company night out or team trip – lasting memories which become part of the organization's 'story book'
16. Talk about top five films, songs etc...
17. Brighten up your environment.
18. Take proper breaks – helps revitalize and refresh, making you more productive in the long run.
20. Organize birthday celebrations.
24. Arrange after-work events such as bowling, ice skating or theatre trips.
26. Share around invitations to networking events.
27. Train for a charity race/event together.
28. Get outside – take a 10-15 minute walk with the team, even having a 'walk and talk' meeting.
29. Have a 'glass half-full' attitude at all times – positivity makes solving issues much more fun.
30. Start a competition with a small, inexpensive prize; for example, guess the total number of hits on the company website, or number of customer calls in a week.

IF YOU ONLY DO **THREE THINGS:**

1 Focus on the goals and outcomes.
2 Use your strengths to complement those of others.
3 Be flexible and do what you say you will.

| **35** | WHAT YOU NEED TO DO NEXT – **HOW TO GET THE BEST OUT OF THIS BOOK**

This is a pretty short chapter because by now you should have started acting upon at least some of the advice in this book.

This is the sort of book you should hang onto. Scribble in it, stick post-its in it, turn the page corners down. Keep referring back to it whenever you have a work challenge or need a bit of a boost.

Encourage your friends and family, your colleagues and, yes, maybe even your manager to read this book.

Use it to help you progress, to keep you on the right track, to give you confidence and maybe even to keep you a little bit saner.

Think of it as a trusted old friend.

In fact, this is more than just a book; it's a whole change of mindset, a movement if you like. You can always email me; jane@purplecubed.com, follow me on Twitter @janesunley or visit www.janesunley.com for free stuff.

And there's more to come; but that would be telling...

Lastly...

BE BRAVE, STRONG AND DETERMINED – ENJOY YOUR JOB, ENJOY LIFE; MOST OF ALL, **ENJOY BEING YOU.**

IF YOU ONLY DO
THREE THINGS FROM THIS
ENTIRE BOOK:

1 Be aware of the importance of culture and values – find a working environment where you can survive and thrive.
2 Put the effort in towards becoming the best 'you' you can be.
3 Be a good, positive person – what goes around comes around.

| **36** | WHY LISTEN **TO ME?**

Everyone has a right to be happy and fulfilled at work,
yet every day I meet or read about people who simply dislike
their jobs or their employers. These are good people with
masses of capabilities and potential. They're in the wrong role/
company/team/place and either aren't confident enough or
don't know how to make the changes necessary to improve
their lives.

People allow this to go on for years. And years…

Some of these people work at very senior or highly skilled
levels, earning big bucks and with very high levels of
responsibility, others less so. This book is intended to provide
some of the inspiration and practicalities towards making the
required changes. This is not a fluffy, new-age self-help book
(though some of them could certainly support the process if
that's your thing). This book is full of practical how-tos; lots of
uncommon, common sense; it is easy to follow and, above all, it
is intended for anyone in any circumstance. However, the onus
is on the reader to take the action – start small, try stuff out, get
some results, then do more…

As an employer both in SMEs and a corporate environment,
I've employed hundreds of people over the years. I love my
people (though not in a weird way) and do what it takes to
help them succeed. In return, they do a fantastic job for me.
This is how work should be and it has never been truer than at
Purple Cubed, which I founded in 2001. We help cool brands,
start-ups and growth brands to be great places to work and thus
become more profitable through their people. Part of our remit
is to advise these organizations on getting the best from their
employees and this is a two-way street, hence this book.

Employers sometimes complain about the way their employees behave – I have to tell you that when questioning the employer, the conclusion is usually that this is to do with the way they treat their people. An old friend of mine used to say: "There are no bad employees, only bad managers" – one to think about. As you might expect, I love my job. I know that people do need help, though, to be able to become a great employee, and much of this is shared within these pages; even some of my own life lessons.

I'm a great observer of people and, living in London, overhear fascinating conversations during my commute to work/in the gym/in restaurants and elsewhere. Much of this is work related and not always very positive.

I originally thought of calling this book 'How Not To Hate Your Job' but then thought better of it, as it's far too negative a title. Hate is a strong word and I hope you never have to use it.

I'm also involved in a brilliant charity called The Brokerage, which helps bright, young, inner-City London residents (many of whom are disadvantaged or from non-privileged backgrounds) into City roles. I'm talking investment banking, law, financial services and so on. Imagine how great it is to see a streetwise hustler from a deprived area of London earning a six-figure salary on the dealing floor of an international investment bank. Over the years, The Brokerage has proven time and time again that anything is possible with the right attitude and approach.

I'm a visiting fellow with both Sheffield Hallam and Oxford Brookes Universities and therefore meet and advise loads of great students. Something that happened one day prompted me to write this book and gave me its title. A job-seeking master's degree student asked me if it was OK to kiss the interviewer (my emphatic response was "No, never, under any circumstances"…!). People like this (and I thank that guy) need to know the basics, so here they are. I also mentor and have mentored many students, young people who are starting out in their careers or maybe in their first or second roles as well as executives and others that are further along the career superhighway. When it comes down to it, they have many issues in common. In my experience, there is so little knowledge around what works and how to show themselves in the best light. I know how people need to behave to be successful and I therefore decided to write down all the advice imparted over the years that has helped people achieve really outstanding results. This stuff is do-able. For anyone.

Lastly, I have two teenage daughters and as a consequence generally have a house full of young people from whom I learn a broad span of fascinating information (not all of it printable). People have so much potential and start out with so much hope; it's important they're able to realize it.

LEADERS

AT ALL LEVELS

Why you need to turn leadership **on its head**

Most organisations apply traditional ways of leading their teams; models and techniques honed over the past 50 years or so. And therein lies the challenge. The world has changed. Much of the leadership and management theory we rely on now was written more than 20 years ago. While on the face of it, some of this still rings true, its sustainability for the future comes into question. There's no doubting there's some very good stuff out there, however the world is a very changed place since Douglas McGregor (the American social psychologist, who introduced his X-Y motivation theory in his book 'The Human Side Of Enterprise', first published in 1960) was a boy. How this information and ideas need to evolve is what Leaders at all Levels is concerned with. I want to help organisations, large and small, to start making the transition now, while there's just about enough time to stay ahead of the game. This might sound simple though the best routes to change often have to be.

Typically the elite executives at the top are developed, coached and encouraged to become charismatic and powerful leaders. They're sent off on massively expensive development programmes. And there's nothing wrong with that, though there's often a disparity. The real experts – those on the front line possess and acquire vast amounts of knowledge and real life know-how, for example when it comes to actually delivering the company's product and service experiences to its customers. They live and breathe market information – official as well as unofficial - and generally have a firm grip on

> The CEO who dons a disguise to work alongside the front line can't be the only one to recognise what's going wrong. The issue is that he or she may well be the only one with the power, freedom and drive to be able to do something about them. Therein lies the heart of the matter.

what's actually happening in real time. That's why 'Back to the Floor' type programmes on TV are so entertaining, revealing and, unfortunately, frequently so perturbing.

And then there's the murky middle management layer. These are the aspiring executives and leaders, who've frequently been promoted from the ranks, often without the development and support to make this, perhaps the most difficult transition of all, successfully. They hold inestimable levels of responsibility and potential impact. They manage their teams and interact with customers. They generally have pressures coming from all sides and often aren't equipped to adequately deal with them; they have no time to think. They are a key communication channel though often messages (both ways don't get through – hence the murkiness.

To the person further down the ranks who reports to the middle manager, this person IS the organisation. Hence the middle manager holds a huge obligation when it comes to engagement, development, motivation, productivity and overall happiness (more about that later).

→HERE'S A SIMPLE (AND, SADLY, TRUE AND NOT ALL THAT UNUSUAL) **STORY:**

Based on the recommendations of a renowned headhunter and a series of successful interviews, the executive team employed a new operations director (OD). The front line teams (those doing the job every day) knew of the approved candidate by reputation from those working under him in his previous company, and it wasn't at all positive.

The front liners attempted to caution the middle managers. Not wanting to question the wisdom of the executives, the managers supported the appointment, telling people they would 'just have to work with it', that they shouldn't form opinions based on gossip and certainly not question the capability of the executive team. By then the decision was made and everyone decided to take a positive approach and make the best of the situation. Though clearly, amongst the ranks, there was an underlying perception that this was not a good appointment.

All went well for a while, the middle managers gave a sigh of relief and business resumed as usual. Honeymoon (induction) period over, the new OD began to set about transforming the business in earnest; earning his stripes, making his mark. In all the wrong ways. The middle managers supported the new OD, fearing for their jobs and wanting to do 'the right thing'. The front liners quickly became disengaged, less productive and many of them left the business. In days gone by, people may well have 'put up and shut up' but today's employee knows that talented people will always have choices.

To cut a long and painful story short, the organisation eventually understood that the OD's appointment had been a poor one and, wanting a swift and low profile resolution, paid him off with a six-figure sum (yes really). They then had to set about repairing the damage. Cost to the business? Probably into seven figures.

By the way, I don't have anything against executives – I am one and I certainly know some impressive types ; it's just important t to make sure a very valuable source of highly relevant, specialist information and expertise – their people – is listened to. In my view it's all about balance...

This is why things need to change. If your organisation isn't maximizing the positive effects and potential of its middle managers and those on the front line, then you're missing out in a big way. The middle management layer should be a vibrant conduit for idea generation, for nurturing, providing support, developing trust and personifying the company's culture. The people should be confident, trusted experts with attitude, skills and knowledge in abundance to be able to deliver the strategy that will make your organisation great.

Ask yourself now, hand on heart, is this the case within your organisation / site / team / you? If not read on...

Why do those at the top so often fail to access the rich seam of information and knowledge the rest of the organisation possesses?

Why do they leave middle managers to find their way without adequate development, support, freedom, trust?

And THE BIG QUESTION:

How can organisations gain from maximising the potential of ALL of their people and over time build up a talent pool that includes everyone?

The answers lie within this book...

➔If you only do three things:
1. Be open minded.
2. Think about leadership –
   does yours really work (at all levels)?
3. Imagine a new world where you were
   'leading' the way.

Pre-publication extract from Leaders at all Levels, *by Jane Sunley, to be released in Autumn 2014.*

BEYOND
THE WRITTEN WORD

Authors who speak to you face to face.

Discover LID Speakers, a service that enables businesses to have direct and interactive contact with the best ideas brought to their own sector by the most outstanding creators of business thinking.

- A network specialising in business speakers, making it easy to find the most suitable candidates.

- A website with full details and videos, so you know exactly who you're hiring.

- A forum packed with ideas and suggestions about the most interesting and cutting-edge issues.

- A place where you can make direct contact with the best in international speakers.

- The only speakers' bureau backed up by the expertise of an established business book publisher.